POCKET GUIDE

MAMMALS

OF SOUTHERN AFRICA

CHRIS & MATHILDE STUART

Struik Nature
(an imprint of Random House Struik (Pty) Ltd)
Wembley Square 2, First Floor, Solan Road, Gardens, Cape Town, 8001
PO Box 1144, Cape Town, 8000 South Africa

Visit **www.randomstruik.co.za** and join the Struik Nature Club
for updates, news, events, and special offers.

First published 2011

3 5 7 9 10 8 6 4

Publishing manager: Pippa Parker
Managing editor: Helen de Villiers
Editor: Colette Alves
Design director: Janice Evans
Designer: Jennifer Addington
Proofreader: Glynne Newlands

Reproduction by Hirt & Carter Cape (Pty) Ltd
Printed and bound by Times Offset (M) Sdn Bhd, Malaysia

ISBN 978 1 77007 861 1

Also available in:
Afrikaans: *Sakgids: Soogdiere van Suider-Afrika* 978 1 77007 886 4
German: *Taschenführer: Säugetiere Südliches Afrika* 978 1 77007 887 1

Front cover: Lion
Back cover, top to bottom: Giraffe, zebra stripes,
Damara dik-dik, gemsbok
Title page: Giraffe
Opposite: Common warthog

CONTENTS

INTRODUCTION

Southern Africa has more than 350 mammal species, a great diversity of habitats and a wealth of natural beauty. It encompasses both the oldest desert in the world, the Namib, and the well-watered Okavango River Delta, the largest inland delta on Earth. Two great oceans lap the region's shores, the Atlantic to the west and the Indian to the south and east. The region has majestic mountain ranges such as the Drakensberg and Soutpansberg, significant rivers that include the Limpopo, Zambezi, Cunene and Orange (Gariep), and the vast, arid lands of the Kalahari, Namaqualand and the Great Karoo.

Politically, southern Africa consists of **South Africa, Namibia, Botswana, Zimbabwe, Mozambique, Swaziland** and **Lesotho.** However, wildlife has been greatly depleted in Swaziland, and little remains in Lesotho.

The vegetation map (page 6) has been greatly simplified but does indicate seven of the most important vegetation zones across the region. Botswana and Namibia have relatively low human populations and extensive tracts of largely unspoilt habitat still remain. Recent warfare in Mozambique, and civil unrest and instability in Zimbabwe have resulted in considerable reductions in game mammal numbers. However, recently improved levels of protection in Mozambique have increased the populations of antelope and other game species in the country. The subcontinent has a fairly extensive network of national parks, game reserves and private wildlife ranches with a great diversity of habitats and species. In general, the countries of southern Africa have a good record in the field of conservation, but some parts have seen a decline in motivation and finances, and a shortage of adequately trained staff.

This book focuses on the larger, more visible species, but also includes a few of the more unusual species, such as the pangolin, aardvark and porcupine, as well as representatives of the different families and genera of bats, shrews, sengis and smaller rodents. Although not frequently seen, they are nevertheless as interesting and diverse as the larger species, and if you are lucky, you may catch a glimpse of some of these denizens of the skies and undergrowth.

The blue wildebeest's natural range is in the north and northeast of the region.

4

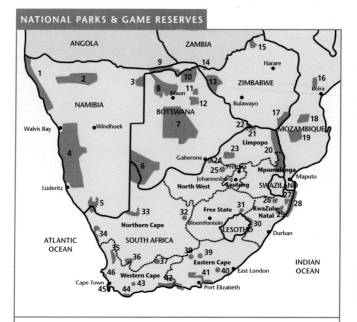

1 Skeleton Coast Park
2 Etosha National Park
3 Khaudom Game Reserve
4 Namib-Naukluft Park
5 Ais-Ais/Richtersveld
   Transfrontier Park
6 Kgalagadi Transfrontier Park
7 Central Kalahari Game Reserve
8 Okavango Delta & Moremi
   Wildlife Reserve
9 Bwabwata National Park
10 Chobe National Park
11 Nxai Pan National Park
12 Makgadikadi Pans
   Nature Reserve
13 Hwange National Park
14 Zambezi National Park
15 Mana Pools National Park
16 Gorongoza National Park
17 Gonarezhou National Park
18 Zinave National Park
19 Banhine National Park
20 Kruger National Park
21 Mapungubwe National Park
22 Tuli Complex
23 Marakele National Park

24 Madikwe Game Reserve
25 Pilanesberg Game Reserve
26 Ithala Game Reserve
27 uMkhuze Game Reserve
28 iSimangaliso Wetland Park
29 Hluhluwe-Imfolozi Game Reserve
30 uKhahlamba Wilderness Complex
31 Golden Gate Highlands
   National Park
32 Mokala National Park
33 Augrabies National Park
34 Namaqua National Park
35 Cedarberg Wilderness Area
36 Tankwa National Park
37 Karoo National Park
38 Camdeboo National Park
39 Mountain Zebra National Park
40 Great Fish River
   Conservation Area
41 Greater Addo Elephant
   National Park
42 Garden Route National Park
43 Bontebok National Park
44 Agulhas National Park
45 Table Mountain National Park
46 West Coast National Park

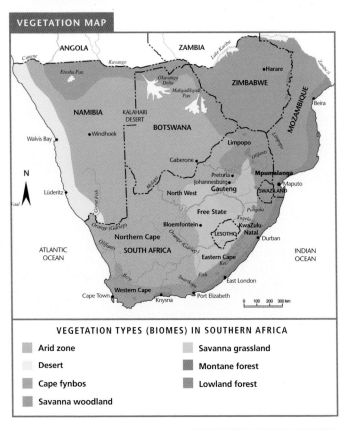

VEGETATION TYPES (BIOMES) IN SOUTHERN AFRICA

- Arid zone
- Desert
- Cape fynbos
- Savanna woodland
- Savanna grassland
- Montane forest
- Lowland forest

Arid (semi-desert) zone

These areas receive higher rainfall than true desert, but rarely more than 500 mm per year. Rocky plains, low, woody shrubs and succulents in the south; sandy soils with low trees and bushes, good grass in the north.

Desert

This biome receives very little rainfall (less than 100 mm per year) and has sparse plant growth. Large areas may be covered by sand dunes or consist of flat gravel plains, devoid of vegetation.

Cape fynbos

Restricted to the Western and Eastern Cape, this zone is rich in plant species and is dominated by evergreen shrubs and bushes.

Savanna woodland

This biome includes mopane woodland, thorn scrub (thicket) and dense woodland habitats in the east. Grass cover ranges from sparse to good.

Savanna grassland

Savanna grassland consists of mixed grassland, with tree and shrub growth more or less restricted to the edges of watercourses and to hills and more rugged terrain.

Montane forest

This forest type occurs at higher altitudes. It is restricted, in fragmented and widely scattered patches, and consists of dense woodland with large trees forming a closed canopy.

Lowland forest

Lowland forest is confined to low altitudes along the eastern coastal plain. It consists of dense, evergreen vegetation with thick undergrowth and some tall trees.

HOW TO USE THIS GUIDE

Information is compiled with a view to easy identification of the larger and more conspicuous mammals of southern Africa, as well as a few of the less frequently seen, yet distinctive, species.

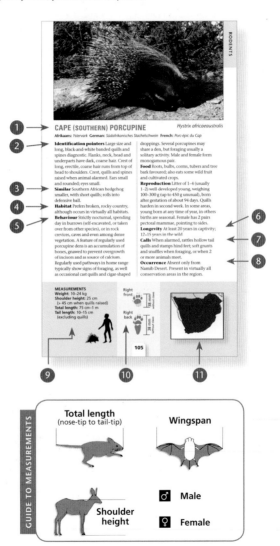

CAPE (SOUTHERN) PORCUPINE

Hystrix africaeaustralis

Afrikaans: *Ystervark* **German:** *Südafrikanisches Stachelschwein* **French:** *Porc-épic du Cap*

Identification pointers Large size and long, black-and-white banded quills and spines diagnostic. Flanks, neck, head and underparts have dark, coarse hair. Crest of long, erectile, coarse hair runs from top of head to shoulders. Crest, quills and spines raised when animal alarmed. Ears small and rounded; eyes small.

Similar Southern African hedgehog smaller, with short quills; rolls into defensive ball.

Habitat Prefers broken, rocky country, although occurs in virtually all habitats.

Behaviour Strictly nocturnal, spending day in burrows (self-excavated, or taken over from other species), or in rock crevices, caves and even among dense vegetation. A feature of regularly used porcupine dens is an accumulation of bones, gnawed to prevent overgrowth of incisors and as source of calcium. Regularly used pathways in home range typically show signs of foraging, as well as occasional cast quills and cigar-shaped

droppings. Several porcupines may share a den, but foraging usually a solitary activity. Male and female form monogamous pair.

Food Roots, bulbs, corms, tubers and tree bark favoured; also eats some wild fruit and cultivated crops.

Reproduction Litter of 1–4 (usually 1–2) well developed young, weighing 100–300 g (up to 450 g unusual), born after gestation of about 94 days. Quills harden in second week. In some areas, young born at any time of year, in others births are seasonal. Female has 2 pairs pectoral mammae, pointing to sides.

Longevity At least 20 years in captivity; 12–15 years in the wild

Calls When alarmed, rattles hollow tail quills and stamps hind feet; soft grunts and snuffles when foraging, or when 2 or more animals meet.

Occurrence Absent only from Namib Desert. Present in virtually all conservation areas in the region.

MEASUREMENTS
Weight: 16–24 kg
Shoulder height: 25 cm
(>45 cm when quills raised)
Total length: 75 cm–1 m
Tail length: 10–15 cm
(excluding quills)

Right front

Right back

38 mm without claws

38 mm without claws

105

GUIDE TO MEASUREMENTS

Total length
(nose-tip to tail-tip)

Wingspan

Shoulder height

♂ Male

♀ Female

8

❶ Name: The common English and scientific names are given, as well as those in Afrikaans, German and French.

❷ Identification pointers: Provides a summary of the animal's most distinctive features.

❸ Similar: Provides names of similar species, or those in the region with which the species is confused, and highlights distinguishing characters.

❹ Habitat: Describes the terrain in which the animal lives; an important aid in identifying a mammal, especially in conjunction with the map.

❺ Behaviour, Food and Reproduction: These are added for interest, but also aid identification. If a species is known to be solitary and you think you have seen it in a herd, read through the text describing behaviour in order to establish an alternative identity.

❻ Longevity: Information on how long the species is known to live.

❼ Calls: The most frequently heard calls are given.

❽ Occurrence: The major parks and reserves in which a species occurs, its conservation status and numbers, if known.

❾ Measurements: Those of male and female are given separately where they differ significantly. Measurements and weights give either known range, or averages, but there may be considerable variations. Also includes silhouette drawings of the species, with that of a human figure, arm or hand for comparison of scale. For so-called 'trophy' species, we have given the Rowland Ward records for southern Africa, but for some we have given those for East Africa and Africa as a whole, where more comprehensive records are available. Larger specimens may be known from beyond the region and these records change on a fairly regular basis.

❿ Tracks: Drawings of typical tracks (where available) add interest and serve as tools for species identification, as do the dung images in the back of the book. Light grey areas on the tracks show only on soft ground.

⓫ Maps: Illustrate range across which the species occurs (red), and the historical distribution (pale tint); marine mammal concentrations (pp. 130-134) are shown in dark blue.

NOTE

SUCCESSFUL MAMMAL WATCHING

To best observe the mammals covered in this guide you will require a pair of binoculars. Once you have spotted a mammal, try to establish the group to which it belongs – is it a type of cat or a dog or an antelope? If possible, estimate height at shoulder level, or guess total length in relation to the tail – is the tail the same length as the head and body, or is it shorter? Are there any outstanding features, such as a bushy tail, spots, stripes or particularly long ears? In the case of an antelope, be sure to note the shape of the horns, and whether they are smooth, strongly ridged or only partly ringed. Remember that young animals may in some cases resemble adults of another species, particularly when seen in stages of early horn development. Make a note of any particular behavioural traits or peculiarities. Was the animal in a group or solitary? Was it in a tree? Did it run down a burrow?

Look out for spoor, or tracks, most easily seen in mud or fine sand. Fresh tracks may give insight into an animal's activities, even if it has not been sighted. Likewise, an animal's droppings provide a useful indicator of its presence – see the dung identification section on page 135.

SOUTHERN LESSER GALAGO (BUSHBABY)

Galago moholi

Afrikaans: *Nagapie* **German:** *Steppengalago* **French:** *Galago mignon*

Identification pointers Small, with long, well-haired tail. Large, mobile, thin ears; large, forward-facing eyes. White under chin, with a lighter coloured stripe running the length of the short, pointed muzzle. Coat is fine, woolly, greyish to grey-brown in colour, with paler underparts (sometimes tinged orange-brown).

Similar Much smaller than thick-tailed galago. Grant's galago (*Galagoides granti*), which occurs across length of Mozambique plain, is slightly larger with browner coat, and lands on all 4 feet, or on front feet; southern lesser lands on hind feet first.

Habitat Occurs in woodland savanna, particularly where acacia trees are present. Will penetrate into more open areas along wooded watercourses.

Behaviour Strictly nocturnal, mainly arboreal, but occasionally descends to the ground to forage. Lives in family groups of 2–8 individuals. Several females spend the day together in a leaf nest or tree holes. Emerges at night to forage alone, but group keeps contact with chattering calls. Group territories of about 3 ha are defended by all troop members, who mark range by urinating on underside of hands and feet. Despite small size, can execute impressive leaps.

Food Tree resin, some wild fruit, insects, other invertebrates and occasionally lizards, small birds and their eggs. There are seasonal and regional dietary differences.

Reproduction 1–2 well-developed young, weighing 9–12 g, born after a 120-day gestation. Births are seasonal, at either end of summer. Female has 1 pair pectoral, 1 pair inguinal mammae.

Longevity 14 years in captivity.

Calls Very vocal. A *chek-chek* call, low croaks, chittering and grunts are common. High whistle when greatly alarmed.

Occurrence Kruger, Marakele, Madikwe (South Africa); Etosha, Caprivi, Khaudom (Namibia); Okavango, Moremi, Chobe, Tuli/Mashatu (Botswana); Hwange, Mana Pools, Gonarezhou (Zimbabwe).

MEASUREMENTS
Weight: 120–210 g
Total length: 30–40 cm
Tail length: 20–25 cm

Right front

30 mm

THICK-TAILED (GREATER) GALAGO
Otolemur crassicaudatus

Afrikaans: *Bosnagaap* **German:** *Riesengalago* **French:** *Galago à queue épaisse*

Identification pointers Largest of the galagos, with large, thin ears and large, forward-facing eyes. Fur is soft and dense, grey to grey-brown with paler to off-white underparts. Tail is long-haired and bushy. Quite commonly moves on the ground, with rump obviously higher than shoulders and long tail usually held erect.

Similar Southern lesser galago and Grant's galago (*Galagoides granti*) much smaller.

Habitat Prefers dense, dry woodland and riverine forest, but also occurs in montane forests, such as in the Soutpansberg.

Behaviour Strictly nocturnal, spending the day in self-constructed nests or among dense vegetation tangles. They rest together in groups of 2–6 individuals, but forage alone at night. A home range has several day-resting sites. Groups usually consist of females and their young, with males in adjacent and overlapping home ranges. Each group forages within a fixed home range, which they mark with urine, and secretion from a chest gland. May occur in large numbers and at high density in suitable habitat. Spends more time on ground than southern lesser galago.

Food Mainly wild fruit and tree resin (particularly acacia), but also insects, other invertebrates and occasional birds and reptiles.

Reproduction Usually 2 (very rarely 3) young, weighing 50–70 g, born after gestation of about 130 days. Births take place just before the rainy season from August to November. Female has 1 pair pectoral, 1 pair inguinal mammae.

Longevity Up to 14 years in captivity.

Calls One of African woodland's most distinctive nocturnal calls: loud, croaking scream, often repeated, especially after dusk and before dawn. Has been likened to call of human baby in distress.

Occurrence Restricted to east of the region. Mapungubwe, Kruger, Ndumo, uMkhuze, Hluhluwe-Imfolozi (South Africa); Mana Pools, Gonarezhou (Zimbabwe); Banhine, Gorongoza, Niasa (Mozambique).

MEASUREMENTS
Weight: 1–1.5 kg
Total length: 70–80 cm
Tail length: 35–45 cm

Right back

50 mm

SAVANNA (CHACMA) BABOON *Papio (hamadryas) cynocephalus*

Afrikaans: *Savannebobbejaan* **German:** *Steppenpavian* **French:** *Babouin cynocéphale*

Identification pointers Largest primate in the region, with relatively slender and long-limbed build. 'Broken', inverted 'U'-shaped tail diagnostic. Elongated, dog-like muzzle is particularly well developed in male. Overall colour and hair length variable, but individuals in south of range tend to be dark grey with longish, shaggy coat; individuals in north are usually more grey-brown with shorter coat. Short hair on upper surfaces of feet and hands is dark brown to black.

Similar No similar primate in the region; see vervet and Sykes's monkeys.

Habitat Wooded savanna, mountain and hilly country; access to drinking water essential. Penetrates arid areas along river courses.

Behaviour Diurnal, retreating to secure roosts for the night. Highly social, living in troops of 15–100 individuals. Males over 5 years of age are dominant over females and there is a strict pecking order. Only dominant males mate with receptive females. Dominant male dictates the troop's movement and when and where it will rest. Females and infants remain closest to this male; non-breeding females stay closer to subordinate males. Youngsters and subadults circulate edges of the troop.

Food True omnivore, feeding on a wide range of plant and animal food. Actively hunts, especially adult male; prey includes young antelope, hares and game birds. Digs for roots, bulbs and insects.

Reproduction Single, pink-faced young, weighing about 1–1.5 kg, born after gestation of about 180 days. Clings to chest hair of mother for first few weeks of life; later rides jockey-fashion on her back. Births occur any time of year. Female has 1 pair pectoral mammae.

Longevity At least 30 years in captivity.

Calls Very vocal; far-carrying bark, or *bogum*, grunting, chattering, squealing and screaming.

Occurrence In many national parks and other conservation areas, also on farmland.

MEASUREMENTS
Weight: ♂ 25–45 kg;
♀ 12–28 kg
Shoulder height: 40–75 cm
Total length: ♂ 1.2–1.8 m;
♀ 1–1.2 m
Tail length: 60–85 cm

Right hand — 79 mm

Right foot — 137 mm

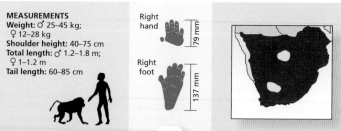

VERVET MONKEY

Cercopithecus pygerythrus

Afrikaans: *Blouaap* **German:** *Südliche Grünmeerkatze* **French:** *Singe vert*

Identification pointers Typical monkey-like appearance, with long tail and black face with white brow-band. Coat is grizzled-grey, sometimes with yellowish-olive infusion. Underparts are paler to white, upper surfaces of hands and feet usually darker to black, but lighter in some populations. Male has powder blue scrotum. Six races in the region doubtfully recognized.

Similar Sykes's monkey much darker, more arboreal.

Habitat Savanna and riverine woodland, often penetrating into arid areas along watercourses. Has recently spread into Great Karoo, where highly terrestrial. Found in coastal scrub and thicket, seldom in forest.

Behaviour Diurnal. Spends great deal of time moving and foraging on ground, but also feeds and sleeps in trees. Troops of 20, or more, individuals may be seen, but most groups tend to be smaller. Each troop has a clear social ranking, which is strictly maintained. Troops are multi-male and multi-female, with little conflict occurring within the group. Forages within a well-defined home range and will defend it against intruding troops.

Food Wide range of fruit, flowers, leaves, seeds and acacia tree resin, as well as insects and small vertebrates. Will raid bird nests for eggs and nestlings. Can become a serious pest in agricultural areas, taking a wide variety of crops.

Reproduction A single young, weighing 350 g average, born after gestation of about 165 days. Newborns have pink faces. Births may occur at any time of year, but summer peaks occur. Female has 1 pair pectoral mammae.

Longevity Up to 31 years in captivity; about 12 years in the wild.

Calls Quiet coughing and gargling contact calls within troop; harsh chattering and repeated sharp barking when threatened or in boundary conflict with another troop.

Occurrence Usually common, often in close proximity to human settlements.

MEASUREMENTS
Weight: ♂ 4–8 kg; ♀ 3.5–5 kg
Total length: ♂ 1–1.3 m;
♀ 95 cm–1.1 m
Tail length: ♂ 60–75 cm;
♀ 48–65 cm

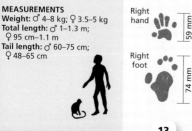

Right hand

Right foot

59 mm

74 mm

SYKES'S (SAMANGO) MONKEY
Cercopithecus albogularis

Afrikaans: *Samango-aap* **German:** *Weißkehlmeerkatze* **French:** *Cercopithèque á collier blanc*

Identification pointers Typical monkey-like appearance. Coat grizzled grey-brown, somewhat browner towards tail base. Black on legs, shoulders and last two-thirds of tail. Long hair on cheeks, white chin and off-white to pale grey underparts. Two subspecies recognized in the region: *C.a. erythrarchus*, with black tail and patches of orange-red on lower buttocks and around anus, occurs from northern KwaZulu-Natal, along escarpment to Soutpansberg and through Mozambique; *C.a. labiatus* has basal third of tail off-white to paler and lacks red patches, occurs in Eastern Cape to KwaZulu-Natal Midlands.

Similar Vervet monkey is pale grizzled-grey, with black face.

Habitat High forest, forest margins and riverine gallery forest; may venture into open woodland. Occupies areas from sea level to mountain forests.

Behaviour Mainly arboreal but does come to the ground to cross clearings and to forage on occasion. During hottest hours rests up in deep shade, but on cool mornings will sit on exposed branches sunning. Forms troops up to 40 strong, although most are smaller. Most troops controlled by single adult male, who will see off other males, but females defend the troop territory. This defence can be vigorous and may result in deaths.

Food Wide range of plants, including fruit, flowers, resin, leaves and seeds.

Reproduction Single young, weighing about 400 g, born after 120–140-day gestation. Most births occur in summer. Female has 1 pair pectoral mammae.

Longevity Up to 20 years, perhaps older, in the wild.

Calls Range of calls, but most obvious is male's loud, far-carrying *jack* or *pyow* call.

Occurrence Isimangaliso, Hluhluwe-Imfolozi, Ndumo, uMkhuze, Ithala, Kruger, Wolkberg, Soutpansberg (South Africa). Occurs in a number of isolated pockets in the east of the region, and has declined in some areas.

MEASUREMENTS
Weight: ♂ 8–10 kg; ♀ 4–5 kg
Total length: ♂ 1.4 m; ♀ 1.2 m
Tail length: ♂ 80 cm; ♀ 70 cm

Right front

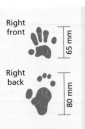

65 mm

Right back

80 mm

PLAINS ZEBRA

Equus quagga

Afrikaans: *Vlaktesebra* **German:** *Steppenzebra* **French:** *Zèbre des plaines*

Identification pointers Stocky, pony-like wild horse with black-and-white stripes extending to underparts, but with minimal or no striping on lower legs. Most populations in the region have light brown to greyish-brown 'shadow' stripes over the white stripes, but in some areas these may be lacking. Mane stands erect (with hair tufts alternately black and white and coinciding with stripes on neck), extending from top of head to shoulders. Ears quite short and tail short-haired near base, with longer hairs towards tip.

Similar Cape and Hartmann's mountain zebras where ranges overlap.

Habitat Grassland plains and open wooded savanna, with access to water.

Behaviour May feed at any time. Small family herd led by a stallion, with usually 4–6 mares and their foals. Although much larger herds are regularly seen, these gatherings are temporary and the family units retain their integrity. Unattached stallions join together in bachelor herds, or run alone.

In larger conservation areas, such as Etosha and central Kalahari, some populations are seasonal migrants; other populations remain in one location throughout the year. Frequently mixes with other herding species, such as blue wildebeest and red hartebeest.

Food Grazer, but occasionally browses.

Reproduction Single foal, weighing 30–35 kg, born after gestation of about 375 days. Most births occur in summer, coinciding with onset of the rains, when there is an abundance of fresh grazing. Mare has 1 pair inguinal mammae.

Longevity 40 years in captivity; up to 20 years in the wild.

Calls Repeated barking *kwa-ha-ha*.

Occurrence Still common in a number of conservation areas and extensively reintroduced or introduced to game farms. Principal populations in Etosha (Namibia); Chobe, Makgadikgadi, Central Kalahari (Botswana); Hwange, Gonarezhou (Zimbabwe); Hluhluwe-Imfolozi, Kruger, uMkhuze (South Africa).

MEASUREMENTS
Weight: 290–340 kg
Shoulder height: 1.3 m
Total length: 2.3–3 m
Tail length: 43–56 cm

Right front

Right back

77 mm

83 mm

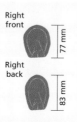

15

1

■ CAPE MOUNTAIN ZEBRA
HARTMANN'S MOUNTAIN ZEBRA

Equus zebra zebra
Equus zebra hartmannae

Afrikaans: *Kaapse bergsebra, Hartmann-bergsebra* **German:** *Kap-Bergzebra, Hartmann-Bergzebra*
French: *Zèbre de montagne du Cap, Zèbre de montagne de Hartmann*

Identification pointers: Pony-like appearance, with black-and-white stripes (but no 'shadow' stripes) and leg striped to hoof. White belly, distinctive 'gridiron' pattern of stripes on rump, throat with dewlap. Tip of muzzle black with orange-brown hair above. Two barely distinguishable subspecies: Hartmann's differs in being slightly larger and has marginally different striping pattern on rump.

Similar Could only be confused with plains zebra.

Habitat Mountainous and broken hill country, but makes frequent use of upland plateaux and adjacent flatland.

Behaviour Diurnal and nocturnal. Mature stallion controls small harem group of up to 4 or 5 mares with their latest young. Hartmann's may form temporary congregations of 40 or more individuals at water, or in areas with good grazing,

but harem group integrity is maintained. Non-harem holding stallions form bachelor groups, which may also include young mares and weaned foals of both sexes. Stallions do not defend territories, but keep other stallions away from mares, although submissive males are tolerated.

Food Predominantly a grazer.

Reproduction Single foal, weighing about 25 kg, born after gestation of some 360 days. Cape may drop young at any time, but has summer peak; most Hartmann's births recorded in Etosha take place in summer. Female has 1 pair inguinal mammae.

Longevity 26 years in captivity.

Calls Snort and high-pitched alarm call from herd stallions.

Occurrence Cape: Mountain Zebra, Karoo, Camdeboo, Bontebok, De Hoop, Gamka (South Africa). **Hartmann's:** Etosha, Namib-Naukluft, Fish River (Namibia).

MEASUREMENTS
Weight: Cape 250–260 kg
  Hartmann's 250–300 kg
Shoulder height: Cape 1.3 m
  Hartmann's 1.5 m
Total length: 2.7 m
Tail length: 40 cm

Right front

100 mm

Right back

100 mm

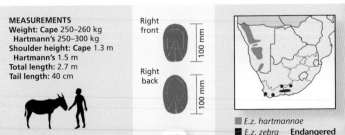

■ *E.z. hartmannae*
■ *E.z. zebra* **Endangered**

HOOK-LIPPED (BLACK) RHINOCEROS
Diceros bicornis

Afrikaans: *Swartrenoster* **German:** *Spitzmaulnashorn* **French:** *Rhinocéros à gueule pointu*

Identification pointers Characteristic large size, no hump on neck, pointed upper lip and 2 pointed horns on face, one above the other. Head held well above ground level when walking. Often called 'black' rhinoceros, but only appears this colour when wet or having rolled in fresh mud. Normal coloration varying shades of grey.

Similar Larger square-lipped (white) rhinoceros has hump on shoulders; large head held close to ground when walking.

Habitat Strong preference for woodland with average height of 4 m, and access to water. In some areas occupies semi-desert and more open country.

Behaviour Diurnal and nocturnal. Spends warmer daylight hours lying up in dense bush; more difficult to observe than square-lipped rhinoceros. Largely solitary, although several may gather at a waterhole. Bull and cow usually only come together to mate. Calf accompanies its mother until 2–4 years old. Lives in established home range that may overlap those of several other individuals. Bulls establish dominance hierarchy by display and fighting, but do not hold a territory.

Food Browse forms bulk of diet, but very selective about what it eats. Twigs neatly bitten off by sharp-edged cheek-teeth. Also takes leaves, flowers, fruit and pods. Fresh, green grass may be eaten.

Reproduction Single calf, weighing about 40 kg, born after about 450-day gestation. Calf walks beside or behind mother. Births take place at any time of year. Female has 1 pair inguinal mammae.

Longevity Up to 45 years on record in captivity; probably > 40 years in the wild.

Calls Snort, wheeze, squeal, grunt and will utter a high-pitched scream. Mostly quiet.

Occurrence Conservation efforts, especially in South Africa and Namibia, brought this species back from the brink of extinction. Most important populations in Kruger, Hluhluwe-Imfolozi, Great Fish River (South Africa); Etosha (Namibia). Recently reintroduced to Okavango Delta.

MEASUREMENTS
Weight: 800–1 100 kg
Shoulder height: 1.6 m
Total length: 3.5–4.3 m
Tail length: 70 cm
Record front horn length:
1.05 m (South Africa)

Right front

Right back

200 mm

190 mm

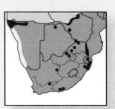

Endangered

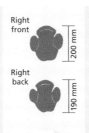

SQUARE-LIPPED (WHITE) RHINOCEROS · *Ceratotherium simum*

Afrikaans: *Witrenoster* **German:** *Breitmaulnashorn* **French:** *Rhinocéros à gueule large*

Identification pointers Massive, square-muzzled head always held close to ground. Diagnostic are obvious hump on shoulder region, large pointed ears and 2 horns, one above the other, on front of face. Name 'white' (from Dutch for 'wide', a reference to broad mouth) is unfortunate as rarely this colour; usually takes on colour of mud in which it wallows.

Similar Hook-lipped rhinoceros smaller, with pointed (not square) upper lip, and usually differs in habitat choice.

Habitat Preference shown for short-grass savanna with areas of thick bush to provide cover and proximity to water for drinking and wallowing.

Behaviour Diurnal and nocturnal. Rests in shade during hotter daylight hours, most feeding taking place during cooler morning and late afternoon. Often seen in loosely knit groups and more social than hook-lipped rhinoceros. Dominant bull in group tolerates other bulls if they remain subservient. Cows occupy home ranges of 6–20 km² that may overlap territories of several bulls. Bull marks edge of its territory with large dung middens, which it visits regularly. Large size and portly demeanor is deceptive, as it can reach a speed of 40 km/h when charging.

Food Selective grazer, with a preference for shorter grasses.

Reproduction Single calf, weighing about 40 kg, born after gestation of some 480 days. Remains with mother for 2–3 years. Calf runs in front of mother, in contrast with hook-lipped rhinoceros. Female has 1 pair inguinal mammae.

Longevity 40–50 years in the wild.

Calls Rumbling growl and deep, bellowing threat call, panting call, squeal and whine, wail and chirping; mostly when in contact with another rhinoceros.

Occurrence Brought to brink of extinction, now numbers almost 18 000, of which majority in South Africa. Reintroduced to all other southern African countries except Lesotho. Largest numbers in Kruger, Hluhluwe-Imfolozi, uMkhuze.

MEASUREMENTS
Weight: ♂ 2 000–2 300 kg; ♀ 1 400–1 600 kg
Shoulder height: 1.8 m
Total length: 4.5–4.8 m
Tail length: 1 m
Record front horn length: 1.58 m

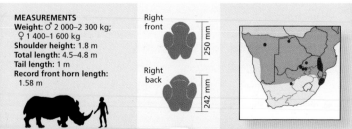

Right front — 250 mm
Right back — 242 mm

COMMON HIPPOPOTAMUS
Hippopotamus amphibius

Afrikaans: *Seekoei* **German:** *Flusspferd* **French:** *Hippopotame*

Identification pointers Large, barrel-shaped body with short, stout legs and massive head with broad muzzle. Skin smooth, hairless and overall greyish-black with pinkish tinge at skin folds and around eyes, ears and mouth. Underparts slightly lighter in colour. Tail short and flattened, with tuft of black bristles at tip.

Similar Should not be mistaken for any other species in the region.

Habitat Shows preference for permanent waters (such as rivers, lakes, marshes and dams) adjacent to grazing grounds.

Behaviour Semi-aquatic, spends most daylight hours in water, but emerges frequently to bask on sand- and mudbanks. Feeds mostly at night, but will graze close to water on cool, overcast days. Travels at night to feeding grounds, which may be as little as a few hundred metres, to several kilometres away. Lives in herds of 10–15 individuals, but larger numbers may gather, each group with a dominant bull. Solitary animals seen are nearly always bulls. Herd bulls mark territories on land with dung, flicked by short tail on to bushes, grass clumps and rocks.

Food Selective grazer, favouring shorter grasses.

Reproduction Mating takes place in water. Single calf, weighing 25–55 kg, born on land, in dense cover, after gestation of 225–257 days. Cow and calf remain apart from herd for several weeks. Birthing any time of year, usually coinciding with rainy season; single peak in southern Africa. Female has 1 pair inguinal mammae.

Longevity 50-61 years in captivity; probably similar in the wild.

Calls Deep. roaring grunts in sequence, snorts, tusk gnashing.

Occurrence Has lost much of its range in South Africa, but occurs in Kruger, Ndumo, uMkhuze, Hluhluwe-Imfolozi and some other reserves, mainly where reintroduced; Caprivi (Namibia); Chobe, Moremi, Okavango (Botswana); Zambezi, Mana Pools, Gonarezhou (Zimbabwe).

MEASUREMENTS
Weight: ♂ 1 000–> 2 000 kg; ♀ 1 000–1 700 kg
Shoulder height: 1.5 m
Total length: 3.4–4.2 m
Tail length: 30–50 cm
Record tusk length (Africa): 163.83 cm

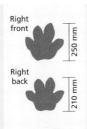

19

COMMON WARTHOG

Phacochoerus africanus

Afrikaans: *Vlakvark* **German:** *Warzenschwein* **French:** *Phacochère commun*

Identification pointers Typical pig-like appearance. Grey, sparsely haired skin takes on colour of mud in which it wallows. Mane of long, erectile hair on neck and back, raised when alarmed. Tufts of white to pale-coloured whiskers along sides of face, especially in younger animals. Male has 2 pairs of prominent, wart-like structures on face, female 1 pair. Canine teeth develop into long, curved tusks beyond upper lip. Tail held erect when running; has tuft of hair at tip.

Similar Bushpig is nocturnal, has dense body hair, lacks long canines, prefers dense habitat, runs with tail held down.

Habitat Open grass and woodland savanna from low to high altitudes, low- and high-rainfall areas.

Behaviour Diurnal, spending nights in burrows either taken over from aardvark or porcupine and modified, or self-excavated. Will also lie up in road culverts. Adult sows form small sounders with their young, but adult boars are normally solitary, or form loose bachelor associations, circulating sounders to test sows for mating readiness. Home range size varies according to food and water availability. Frequent mud-wallowers.

Food Mainly grass and grass roots; also digs for bulbs, corms and rhizomes. Browses on occasion and eats fallen wild fruit. Rarely takes animal food. Often kneels on forelegs when grazing.

Reproduction Litters of 1–8 (usually 2–4) piglets, weighing 480–850 g, born after 170-day gestation. Young remain in, or close to, burrow for first 2 weeks. Breeding possible throughout year, most births occur in summer. Sow has 1 pair inguinal, 1 pair abdominal mammae.

Longevity 17 years (1 record 18 years 9 m) in captivity; probably less in the wild.

Calls Normally silent but will grunt, snuffle and squeal. Young more vocal than adults.

Occurrence Widespread and common across much of the north of the region. Introduced population in Eastern Cape.

MEASUREMENTS
Weight: ♂ 60–105 kg;
♀ 45–70 kg
Shoulder height: 60–70 cm
Total length: 1.3–1.8 m
Tail length: 45 cm
Record tusk length (Africa): 61 cm

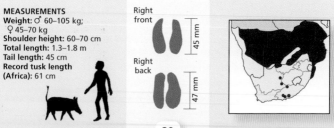

Right front

45 mm

Right back

47 mm

BUSHPIG

Potamochoerus larvatus

Afrikaans: *Bosvark* **German:** *Buschschwein* **French:** *Potamochère*

Identification pointers Pig-like in appearance, well-haired and bristled body with longer mane of hair on neck and shoulders. Head rather long, usually with greyish-white facial mask in adult and ears often with terminal tuft. Overall colour greyish-brown to reddish-brown, but variable. Piglet dark brown with pale longitudinal stripes along body. Tail held down when running.

Similar Common warthog is sparsely haired and usually greyish; holds tail erect when running.

Habitat Dense bush or thicket country, including forest, woodland and reed beds.

Behaviour Mainly nocturnal, but sometimes seen during the day in undisturbed areas. Lives in sounders of 2–15 individuals, sometimes more, usually each with a dominant boar; other boars often solitary. Dominant boar and sow in sounder probably defend a resource territory and boar plays active role in raising and protecting piglets.

Food True omnivore, eats a wide range of plant food and fairly large quantity of animal food. Digs with snout for roots, bulbs and insects, as well as frogs and mice. Scavenges from carcasses of dead mammals. Sometimes, especially during drought, will attack sheep and goats. Can be serious nuisance in croplands.

Reproduction Before farrowing sow constructs 'haystack' of dry grass in which 2–4 (up to 8) piglets, weighing about 750 g, born after 120–130-day gestation. Most births in summer, coinciding with onset of rains. Sow has 3 pairs abdominal mammae.

Longevity Up to 21 years 7 months in captivity; 12–15 years in the wild.

Calls Grunts, squeals and alarm growl.

Occurrence Common, especially in northeast of region. In most parks and reserves within its range, including Kruger, Ndumo, uMkhuze, Hluhluwe-Imfolozi, Great Fish River, Garden Route (South Africa); Chobe, Moremi (Botswana); Mana Pools, Gonarezhou (Zimbabwe).

MEASUREMENTS
Weight: 46–115 kg
(♂ larger than ♀)
Shoulder height: 55–88 cm
Total length: 1.3–1.7 m
Tail length: 38 cm
**Record tusk length
(Africa):** 30.2 cm

Right front

55 mm

Right back

53 mm

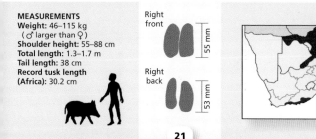

GIRAFFE

Giraffa camelopardalis

Afrikaans: *Kameelperd* **German:** *Giraffe* **French:** *Girafe*

Identification pointers Unmistakable with its immense height, long legs and neck, and back sloping downwards from shoulders to rump. Body covered with lattice pattern of large, irregularly shaded patches separated by networks of light-coloured bands. Both sexes carry a pair of short, blunt horns, usually ringed with black hairs at tip. Two races sometimes recognized, the Angolan and the Cape, but differences small and probably not valid.
Similar Unmistakable.
Habitat Dry savanna woodland, particularly areas dominated by *Acacia*, *Commiphora* and *Terminalia* trees. Avoids dense woodland. Drinking water essential.
Behaviour Feeds during day and at night, but usually rests during hotter hours. Does not establish defended territory, but occupies large home range of usually 20–85 km², but occasionally > 120 km². Usually in herds of 4–30, but groups are unstable, with much intermingling of individuals and herds. Ranges of mature

bulls are smaller than those occupied by cows; young bulls roam widely. Young cows normally remain within mothers' home range, but young bulls disperse in their third or fourth year.
Food Almost exclusively browser. Adult requires about 60 kg of food per day. Tree leaves, flowers, shoots and pods are taken, especially of acacia trees, but shifts to more evergreen species during dry season.
Reproduction Single calf, averaging 100 kg, born after about 450-day gestation. Calf can stand and walk within an hour. Birthing any time of year. Female has 2 pairs inguinal mammae.
Longevity Up to 36 years 2 months in captivity.
Calls Seldom heard; brays under stress, grunts and bellows.
Occurrence Common in larger savanna parks and reserves, rare outside. Kruger, Hluhluwe-Imfolozi, Kgalagadi (South Africa); Etosha (Namibia); Chobe, Central Kalahari (Botswana); Hwange, Gonarezhou (Zimbabwe).

MEASUREMENTS
Weight: ♂ 970–1 400 kg;
♀ 700–950 kg
Shoulder height: ♂ 2.6–3.5 m;
♀ 2–3 m
Total height: ♂ 3.9–5.2 m;
♀ 3.7–4.7 m
Total length:
♂ 4.6–5.7 m; ♀ < 5 m
Tail length:
♂ 96 cm–1.5 m;
♀ 75–90 cm

Right front

180 mm

Right back

170 mm

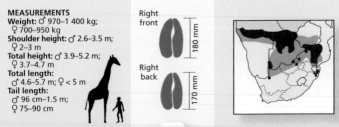

AFRICAN (SAVANNA) BUFFALO

Syncerus caffer

Afrikaans: *Buffel* **German:** *Afrikanischer Büffel* **French:** *Buffle d'Afrique*

Identification pointers Cattle-like appearance, but easily separated from domestic cattle. Massive size, heavily built; short, stocky legs and large, fringed ears that hang below horns. Massive horns form heavy boss, especially in bull, where they meet; tips point inwards. Overall colour dark brown to black, without markings.

Similar Can only be confused with similarly coloured domestic cattle, but see horns.

Habitat Open woodland savanna with abundant grass and drinking water. Will also extend on to open grassland, but only adjacent to bush cover.

Behaviour Much feeding done at night; seeks out shade during hottest hours; will frequently mud-wallow. Usually drinks in early morning and late afternoon. Herds of several score to several thousand individuals, but also solitary and small groups of bulls commonly seen. Mixed herds consist of cows, young of different ages and adult bulls that maintain a dominance hierarchy. Dominant bull, or bulls, will mate with cows in breeding condition. Cows establish a pecking order among themselves. Herds occupy defined home ranges.

Food Mainly grazer, prefers grasses that grow in dense swards. Some browse is taken, mainly in the dry season.

Reproduction Single calf, weighing 30–40 kg, born after gestation of about 340 days. Majority of calves born in wet and warm summer months. Cow has 2 pairs inguinal mammae.

Longevity Up to 29 years 6 months in captivity; 20 years in the wild.

Calls Bellow, calf bleats, 'creaking gate' call, *maaa* (similar to cow *moo*), low grunts and croaks.

Occurrence Restricted to north and east; once more widespread. Greater Addo, Hluhluwe-Imfolozi, uMkhuze, Ithala, Kruger, Marakele, Mapungubwe (South Africa); Gonarezhou, Hwange, Mana Pools, (Zimbabwe); Chobe, Moremi (Botswana); Banhine, Gorongoza, Niasa (Mozambique).

MEASUREMENTS
Weight: ♂ 700 kg; ♀ 550 kg
Shoulder height: 1.4 m
Total length: 2.9 m
Tail length: > 70 cm
Record horn length: 124.8 cm

Right front

Right back

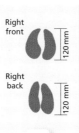

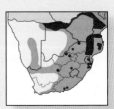

23

COMMON ELAND

Tragelaphus oryx

Afrikaans: *Eland* **German:** *Elenantilope* **French:** *Éland*

Identification pointers Largest antelope in the region, with ox-like appearance. Overall coloration is fawn to tawny-grey, with older animals often more grey on forequarters, neck and face. In far north of region subspecies (*T.o. livingstonii*) has up to 7 vertical, white stripes on each side. Bull develops large, pendulous dewlap on throat and lower neck, and prominent hair tuft on front of face. Both sexes carry shallowly spiralled horns, those of bulls being heavier.

Similar Size and coloration separate it from other species, but see roan antelope and greater kudu.

Habitat Most savanna and open woodland associations, from semi-desert (Kalahari) to high-rainfall areas (Drakensberg), from sea level to higher altitudes.

Behaviour Mainly diurnal, also feeds at night, especially during summer. Usually in herd of 25–60 animals, but larger numbers sometimes gather. Nomadic in Kalahari, but more or less sedentary in other areas, such as Drakensberg. Bulls establish hierarchy that determines mating rights; there appears to be no establishment of territories. Cows develop a hierarchical system, establishing access to feeding sites and position within herd.

Food Mainly browser, but does graze, especially on new growth.

Reproduction Single calf (rarely twins), weighing 22–36 kg, born after gestation of about 270 days. Births any time of year, but a spring/summer birthing peak occurs. Calf remains hidden for first 2 weeks. Cow has 2 pairs inguinal mammae.

Longevity 26 years in captivity; up to 20 years, but usually less, in the wild.

Calls Bleats, loud alarm barks, bellows.

Occurrence Once occurred throughout region, now in conservation areas; widely reintroduced. Main populations in Kruger, Kgalagadi, uKhahlamba (South Africa); Etosha, Khaudom (Namibia); Chobe, Central Kalahari, Makgadikgadi (Botswana); Hwange, Gonarezhou (Zimbabwe).

MEASUREMENTS
Weight: ♂ 700–900 kg; ♀ 450 kg
Shoulder height: ♂ 1.7 m;
  ♀ 1.5 m
Total length: ♂ 3–4.2 m;
  ♀ 2.2–3.5 m
Tail length: 60 cm
Record horn length:
  118.4 cm
  (Namibia)

Right front

100 mm

Right back

85 mm

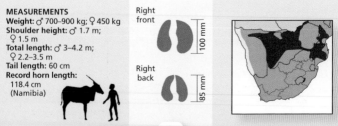

GREATER KUDU

Tragelaphus strepsiceros

Afrikaans: *Koedoe* **German:** *Großer Kudu* **French:** *Grand koudou*

Identification pointers Large, with long legs and short-maned shoulder hump. Overall coat colour grey-brown to rufous, with neck usually greyer than rest of body. Flanks have 6–10 vertical white stripes. Distinct, narrow, white chevron between eyes. Both sexes have shoulder mane, only bulls have fringe of long hair on throat and lower neck. Ears very large and rounded. Bull carries long, deeply spiralled horns, regarded as among the most spectacular of all antelope horns.

Similar Should not be confused, but compare female with smaller nyala ewe.

Habitat Wooded savanna, especially acacia woodland and broken hill country. Penetrates arid areas along wooded watercourses.

Behaviour Active at night and during cooler daylight hours; rests up under cover in hotter hours. Small herds of 3–10 individuals, usually cows and their young. Larger groups may be temporary, but temporary, at either water or favoured feeding sites. Adult bulls circulate freely throughout the year, normally only joining nursery herds during the rut. Small bachelor herds common, but solitary bulls frequently seen. Adept jumper, clearing 2-m fence with ease when pushed.

Food Mainly browses, but will graze, especially on new green grass growth. During drought will eat tree bark, scraped off with incisors. Takes seed pods, especially of *Acacia*, and their blossoms.

Reproduction Single calf, weighing about 16 kg, born after 270-day gestation. No distinct birth season, but summer peak. Calf remains hidden for first 2–3 months. Cow has 2 pairs inguinal mammae.

Longevity 23 years in captivity; 7–8 years average in the wild.

Calls Loud, gruff bark or cough; other sounds made but seldom heard.

Occurrence Widespread in the region; range expanding through arid Karoo. Occurs in all major parks, reserves and numerous private game farms. Abundant in Namibia and Eastern Cape, South Africa.

MEASUREMENTS
Weight: ♂ 250 kg; ♀ 180 kg
Shoulder height: 1.2–1.55 m
Total length: 2.3–2.9 m
Tail length: 43 cm
Record horn length: 187.6 cm (along curve)

Right front
67 mm

Right back
56 mm

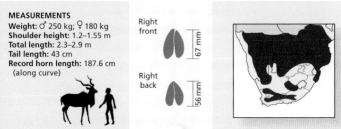

NYALA

Tragelaphus angasii

Afrikaans: *Njala* **German:** *Nyala* **French:** *Nyala*

Identification pointers Sexes markedly different. Ram has fringe of long hair hanging from underparts, from just behind chin to between hind legs, and erectile mane from back of head to rump. Rump and upperparts of hind legs covered with long hair. Between 8 and 14 narrow, vertical, white stripes on each side. Overall slate-grey to dark brown; lower legs rufous to yellow-brown. Shallow 'V'-shaped chevron between eyes. Ewe much smaller, with short-haired coat. Overall colour yellow-brown or chestnut, with up to 18 vertical white body stripes. Only ram carries slightly spiralled horns, tipped with whitish-yellow.
Similar See smaller bushbuck.
Habitat Dry savanna woodland and along watercourses. May graze in open areas adjacent to bush or tree cover.
Behaviour Diurnal and nocturnal. Rams do not hold territories, but rely on elaborate displays to intimidate rivals and establish dominance hierarchies. Commonly seen in groups, nursery herds

of ewes and lambs, bachelor groups and solitary rams. Group composition is fluid and continuously changing, although nursery herds more stable. Larger groups temporary, associated with sought-after food resource or water. Home range size varies from 0.65 km² to almost 4 km².
Food Mainly takes browse but also fresh grass growth on occasion, as well as fallen tree flowers and fruit.
Reproduction A single lamb, weighing 4.2–5.5 kg, born after about 220-day gestation. Births at any time of year, with peaks in spring and early summer. Young remains hidden for first 2 weeks. Ewe has 2 pairs inguinal mammae.
Longevity Up to 14 years in the wild.
Calls Alarm call a harsh bark; ewe makes click-call; lamb bleats.
Occurrence Natural range far east of region and relatively common; widely introduced outside range. Ndumo, uMkhuze, Hluhluwe-Imfolozi, Kruger (South Africa); Gonarezhou (Zimbabwe).

MEASUREMENTS
Weight: ♂ 108 kg; ♀ 62 kg
Shoulder height: ♂ 1.15 m; ♀ 97 cm
Total length: ♂ 2.1 m; ♀ 1.8 m
Tail length: ♂ 43 cm; ♀ 36 cm
Record horn length: 83.5 cm

Right front

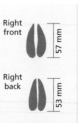

57 mm

Right back

53 mm

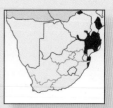

SITATUNGA
Tragelaphus spekei

Afrikaans: *Sitatoenga* **German:** *Sitatunga, Wasserkudu* **French:** *Sitatunga*

Identification pointers Medium-sized antelope with hindquarters higher than shoulders. Coat fairly long and shaggy. Ram is overall grey-brown, with few or no clear markings; ewe is usually more rufous with a few distinct to indistinct vertical, white body stripes. Ram carries long, white-tipped, lightly spiralled horns. Hooves are exceptionally long, an adaptation to semi-aquatic life.

Similar Habitat and appearance should help avoid confusion, but see bushbuck; may feed at night in woodland where smaller bushbuck occur.

Habitat Dense reed beds and well-vegetated aquatic environments, but will feed at night in woodland fringing swamp. May be observed feeding on floating grass islands.

Behaviour Mainly diurnal, but also feeds at night. Common grouping consists of adult ram with several ewes and their young. Solitary rams are common, as are mixed groups of young animals.

Takes readily to water to escape danger or move between feeding sites, and can swim well for long distances. Home ranges are small, this being a measure of the abundance and nutritional richness of their food.

Food Papyrus, reeds, aquatic grasses, but will also graze and browse in adjacent woodland.

Reproduction Single fawn born after gestation of about 220 days. Young can be born at any time of year, but peaks in dry season in the region. Fawn remains hidden for several weeks on platform of trampled reeds. Ewe has 2 pairs inguinal mammae.

Longevity 17–20 years in captivity.

Calls Main call a sharp bark similar to that of bushbuck; repeated.

Occurrence In the region occurs only in Botswana's Okavango Delta and adjacent areas of Caprivi Strip in Namibia. Present in Moremi (Botswana); Caprivi (Namibia).

MEASUREMENTS
Weight: ♂ 115 kg; ♀ 55 kg
Shoulder height:
♂ 88 cm–1.25 m; ♀ 75–90 cm
Total length: ♂ 1.72–1.95 m;
♀ 1.55–1.8 m
Tail length: 22 cm
Record horn length:
92.4 cm

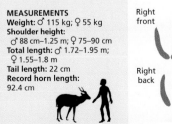

Right front

120–180 mm

Right back

80 mm

♀

♂

BUSHBUCK

Tragelaphus scriptus

Afrikaans: *Bosbok* **German:** *Buschbock, Schirrantilope* **French:** *Guib harnaché*

Identification pointers Smallest of the spiral-horned antelope. Overall colour varies from dark brown to reddish-yellow, and shades between. Vertical white stripes and spots on sides, but very variable. Two white patches on throat. Ram has longish erectile mane on back. Three subspecies recognized in the region: most brightly marked is Chobe bushbuck (*T.s. roualeyni*), darkest is 'Cape' bushbuck (*T.s. sylvaticus*), and intermediate is northeastern *T.s. ornatus*. Southern bushbuck sometimes placed as *T. sylvaticus*. Ram carries short, smooth, shallowly spiralled horns.

Similar Smaller and more clearly marked than sitatunga; compare females of this and nyala – latter has numerous white, vertical body stripes.

Habitat Riverine woodland and bush cover associated with, or close to, water, from sea level to about 3 000 m. Enters open glades and woodland fringes, but never far from cover.

Behaviour Mainly nocturnal, but often feeds during cooler early morning and late afternoon hours. Largely solitary, but loosely knit groups of ewes and lambs commonly seen.

Food Mainly browses on leaves, but also flowers, fruit and shoots.

Reproduction Single fawn, weighing 3.5–4.5 kg, born after 180-day gestation. Fawn lies up in dense cover for up to 4 months. Births can take place any month, but peaks usually coincide with rainy season. Ewe has 2 pairs inguinal mammae.

Longevity > 12 years in captivity; probably 8–9 years in the wild.

Calls Main call a sharp bark.

Occurrence Common and widespread in east and south of region. Garden Route, Greater Addo, Great Fish River, Hluhluwe-Imfolozi, uMkhuze, Ndumo, Kruger, Marakele, Mapungubwe (South Africa); Okavango/Moremi, Chobe (Botswana); Mana Pools, Gonarezhou (Zimbabwe); Banhine, Gorongoza, Niasa (Mozambique).

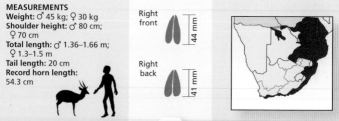

MEASUREMENTS
Weight: ♂ 45 kg; ♀ 30 kg
Shoulder height: ♂ 80 cm;
♀ 70 cm
Total length: ♂ 1.36–1.66 m;
♀ 1.3–1.5 m
Tail length: 20 cm
Record horn length:
54.3 cm

Right front

44 mm

Right back

41 mm

ROAN ANTELOPE

Hippotragus equinus

Afrikaans: *Bastergemsbok* **German:** *Pferdeantilope* **French:** *Antilope rouenne*

Identification pointers Second largest antelope in the region, after common eland. Horse-like, with short, thick neck and distinct, erect mane running from between ears to just beyond shoulders. Conspicuous black-and-white facial markings and long ears tipped with tassel of hair. Overall body colour greyish-brown; underparts paler. Both sexes carry back-curved and heavily ringed horns, those of bull being heavier.

Similar Sable antelope has longer horns and different coat colour; common eland is much bigger, with straight horns.

Habitat Open or lightly wooded grassland with medium-length to tall grasses and access to water. Avoids short-grassed areas.

Behaviour Mainly diurnal, but night activity not unusual. Herd of 5–12 individuals is held by a dominant bull. Bull defends nursery herd (not a territory) against other bulls. Larger herds sometimes seen, but merely temporary gatherings and seldom stable. Herd is usually led by a cow that dominates other cows and selects feeding and resting sites. Young bulls are driven from herds and form bachelor groups; only at 5–6 years do they seek out nursery herds.

Food Grazes, selecting medium-height and long grasses.

Reproduction Single calf, weighing 15–18 kg, born after gestation of about 280 days. Births recorded throughout year. After birth, calf remains hidden for about 2 weeks and is suckled by its mother twice daily. Cow has 2 pairs inguinal mammae.

Longevity 14–17 years in captivity.

Calls Snorts; cow and calf manifest bird-like contact and distress calls; bulls roar during fights.

Occurrence Major declines in range and numbers, even in Kruger. Kruger, Mokala, Pilanesberg (South Africa); Chobe (Botswana); Caprivi, Khaudom, Waterberg, Etosha (Namibia); Hwange, Mana Pools, Gonarezhou (Zimbabwe).

MEASUREMENTS
Weight: 220–300 kg
(♂ heavier than ♀)
Shoulder height: 1.1–1.5 m
Total length: 2.26–2.89 m
Tail length: 54 cm
Record horn length:
99.06 cm
(Zimbabwe)

Right front
120 mm

Right back
120 mm

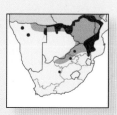

SABLE ANTELOPE

Hippotragus niger

Afrikaans: *Swartwitpens* **German:** *Rappenantilope* **French:** *Hippotrague noir*

Identification pointers Large size, black-and-white facial markings and long, strongly ringed, sabre-like horns diagnostic. Adult bull is overall black, with contrasting white underparts. Cow is usually reddish-brown to chestnut, often darkening with age, with white underparts. Backs of ears in both sexes are brown. Female horns are similar to those of male, but shorter and more slender. Erect, fairly long mane from top of neck to just beyond shoulders.

Similar Roan antelope has shorter horns and differs in coloration.

Habitat Dry, open woodland with medium-length to tall grass; access to water a requirement.

Behaviour Mostly active during cooler morning and late afternoon hours, but also active at night. Usually in herds of 10–30 individuals; large temporary groups sometimes seen. Bull establishes territory that overlaps home ranges of one or more nursery herds. These home ranges are stable and quite small. During the rut, bull tries to hold nursery herds within their territories. Adult cow leads herd, usually directing movements to feeding and resting grounds. Young bulls join bachelor herds until their fifth or sixth year, then move away to establish own territories.

Food Mainly grazes, but browses on occasion, especially in dry season.

Reproduction Single calf, weighing 13–18 kg, born after gestation of about 270 days. Birth season variable, but in most parts of region during summer months. Cow has 2 pairs inguinal mammae.

Longevity 17 years in captivity.

Calls Cow and calf manifest bird-like contact and distress calls; bull roars; both sexes snort.

Occurrence Has suffered declines in range and numbers, including in Kruger. Kruger, Pilanesberg, Marakele, Mapungubwe (South Africa); Chobe (Botswana); Hwange, Gonarezhou, Mana Pools (Zimbabwe). Widely introduced on game farms outside natural range.

MEASUREMENTS
Weight: 180–270 kg
(♂ larger than ♀)
Shoulder height: 1.35 m
Total length: 2.3–2.56 m
Tail length: 50 cm
Record horn length:
140.65 cm

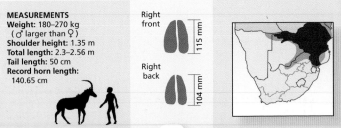

Right front
115 mm

Right back
104 mm

SOUTHERN ORYX (GEMSBOK)

Oryx gazella

Afrikaans: *Gemsbok* **German:** *Spießbock, Oryx* **French:** *Oryx gazelle*

Identification pointers Heavily built, with short, thick neck and distinct black-and-white markings on head, body and legs. Long, black-haired, horse-like tail. Body colour is greyish-fawn, separated from white underparts by black streak along flanks. Black patches on upper part of legs and along top of rump. Black stripe runs down front of neck. Calves are fawn and lack black markings. Both sexes carry long, almost straight, ridged and rapier-like horns; those of bull shorter, stouter.

Similar Roan antelope larger, with scimitar-shaped horns; has similar black-and-white facial markings, but no black on body.

Habitat Open, dry country, also open woodland, grassveld and dune country.

Behaviour Diurnal and nocturnal. Lives in herd of about 15 individuals, sometimes more, particularly during rains. Mixed herd of bulls, cows and calves of different ages, or nursery herd of cows and calves; solitary bulls common. Territorial bull will herd a mixed, or nursery, herd into his territory; he alone will mate with receptive cows. Tends to be nomadic in non-confined areas, moving to fresh vegetation growth stimulated by typically patchy rains.

Food Mainly grazes, but also browses. Also eats seed pods and wild fruit.

Reproduction Single calf, weighing about 15 kg, born after gestation of about 264 days. Births at any time of year, but usually linked to seasonal rainfall. Calf hides and will move with mother at night to new resting site for up to 3 weeks after birth. Cow has 2 pairs inguinal mammae.

Longevity 18–20 years in captivity.

Calls Bulls roar or bellow when fighting; contact grunt, but otherwise silent.

Occurrence Has declined over parts of range but widely reintroduced or introduced. Kgalagadi, Madikwe, Pilanesberg, Richtersveld (South Africa); Central Kalahari, Chobe (Botswana); Hwange (Zimbabwe); Namib-Naukluft, Skeleton Coast, Etosha, Khaudom (Namibia).

MEASUREMENTS
Weight: ♂ 240 kg; ♀ 210 kg
Shoulder height: 1.2 m
Total length: 1.9–2.16 m
Tail length: 46 cm
Record horn length:
125.7 cm (Kalahari)

Right front

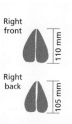

110 mm

Right back

105 mm

COMMON WATERBUCK

Kobus ellipsiprymnus

Afrikaans: *Waterbok* **German:** *Wasserbock* **French:** *Cobe à croissant*

Identification pointers Quite large, with coarse, shaggy, greyish-brown coat, and distinctive white ring circling rump. Only bull carries long, ringed and forward-swept horns. White band usually present on upper throat, with white around muzzle and on lips. Strong, distinctive smell given off by their oily hair.

Similar See reedbuck species, but they are much smaller and lighter coloured, with bushy tails.

Habitat Always associated with water, preferring areas with reed beds or tall grass; also found in woodland. Grazes in open grassland adjacent to cover.

Behaviour Diurnal and nocturnal. Usually in small herds of 5–10 individuals, but up to 30 strong. Larger herds usually seen during rainy season. Young bulls form bachelor herds that usually circulate in areas well away from territory-holding bulls. Adult bull establishes territory through which nursery herds move freely; during the rut he tries to hold cows for mating. Bull establishes own territory at 5 or 6 years of age; once established, it is stable and held until usurped by another bull. Despite elaborate displays by dominant bulls, with young bulls showing subservience, serious fighting is quite common and may result in death.

Food Mainly grasses, but browses on occasion, especially in dry season.

Reproduction Single calf (rarely twins), weighing about 13 kg, born after about 280-day gestation. Calf remains hidden for first 3–5 weeks. Birthing at any time of year, but with summer peak. Cow has 2 pairs inguinal mammae.

Longevity 18 years in the wild, but this is exceptional. Few animals reach 15.

Calls Cow and calf bleat; alarm snort.

Occurrence Natural range in northeast of region but introduced far outside this range. Hluhluwe-Imfolozi, Mapungubwe, uMkhuze, Ndumo, Kruger (South Africa); Chobe, Moremi (Botswana); Hwange, Matobo, Mana Pools, Gonarezhou (Zimbabwe); Gorongoza (Mozambique).

MEASUREMENTS
Weight: 250–270 kg
Shoulder height: 1.3 m
Total length: 2.1–2.74 m
Tail length: 35 cm
Record horn length: 99.7 cm

Right front

Right back

90 mm

90 mm

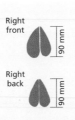

RED LECHWE

Kobus leche leche

Afrikaans: *Letsjwe* **German:** *Litschi, Moorantilope* **French:** *Cobe lechwe*

Identification pointers Hindquarters higher than shoulders; upperparts bright chestnut colour and underparts from chin to belly white. Conspicuous black lines run down front of forelegs. Only ram carries long, strongly ringed, lyre-shaped horns. Longish tail has a tip of black hair.

Similar Puku has less extensive white underparts and lacks dark markings on forelegs; common waterbuck larger and less brightly coloured.

Habitat Flood plains and seasonal swamps; rarely ventures more than 2–3 km from permanent water.

Behaviour Diurnal; active early morning and late afternoon, lies up during heat of day and at night. Water-loving, taking readily to water to feed and when threatened. Usually in herds of up to 30 individuals, but occasionally thousands may gather. Rams form small territories within which they keep small groups of ewes for mating. Small bachelor groups of non-breeding rams congregate on edges of mating grounds. Nursery herds of ewes and young move freely through ram territories, which are very small, rarely exceeding 150 m in diameter. Subservient rams are permitted to pass through these territories as long as they show no interest in ewes. Although quite slow on land, can move rapidly in shallow water, and will swim readily.

Food Semi-aquatic grasses and reeds.

Reproduction Single calf, weighing about 5 kg, born after 225-day gestation. Calf remains hidden for first 2–3 weeks. Most births in Okavango Delta and Chobe from October to December, but some in all months. Ewe has 2 pairs inguinal mammae.

Longevity One captive lived for 15 years; in the wild probably much less.

Calls Communicates with low whistle; alarm whinny-grunt.

Occurrence Has a very limited range in the region. Chobe, Moremi, Okavango Delta (Botswana); Caprivi (Namibia).

MEASUREMENTS
Weight: ♂ 100 kg; ♀ 80 kg
Shoulder height: ♂ 1 m;
♀ 96 cm
Total length: ♂ 1.6 m; ♀ 1.5 m
Tail length: 34 cm
Record horn length: 93.98 cm
(Botswana)

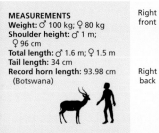

Right front

80 mm

Right back

75 mm

PUKU

Kobus vardonii

Afrikaans: *Poekoe* **German:** *Puku* **French:** *Puku*

Identification pointers Medium-sized, with upperparts golden-brown to yellow-brown, slightly paler sides and off-white underparts. Throat, sides of muzzle and hair around eyes also off-white. Otherwise no distinct markings. Legs uniformly brown. Well-haired tail is golden-yellow with white hairs below. Only ram carries relatively short, stout, lyre-shaped and deeply ringed horns. Some authorities consider puku to be a subspecies of kob, which does not occur in this region.

Similar Common reedbuck has distinct markings and horns differ. Also see lechwe, but that has distinct leg markings, and the rams have much longer horns. Impala has distinguishing markings on rump, is smaller and has lighter build.

Habitat Open flatland adjacent to rivers and marshes, but rarely ventures far onto open flood plain.

Behaviour Diurnal, but some nocturnal activity. Herds of 5–30 individuals, but numbers unstable as movement of individuals between different groups is common. Nursery herds of ewes and young move across territories of several rams. Territories are temporary; usually held for short periods, rarely longer than a few months. Rams attempt to keep nursery herds within their territories and mate with ewes in breeding condition.

Food Predominantly grasses, favouring different species at certain times of year.

Reproduction Single lamb, weighing about 5 kg, born after gestation of some 240 days. Lamb hides in a grass form for first few weeks of life. When lambs join herd they keep together in a crèche. Breeding throughout year, but May–September birth peak. Ewe has 2 pairs inguinal mammae.

Longevity 17 years in captivity.

Calls Distinctive sharp, repeated whistles by territorial rams, also indicating alarm.

Occurrence In the region found only on Pookoo Flats and along Chobe River. Chobe (Botswana); Caprivi (Namibia).

MEASUREMENTS
Weight: ♂ 74 kg; ♀ 62 kg
Shoulder height: 80 cm
Total length: 1.5–1.7 m
Tail length: 28 cm
Record horn length: 56.2 cm

Right front

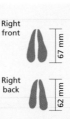

67 mm

Right back

62 mm

MOUNTAIN REEDBUCK

Redunca fulvorufula

Afrikaans: *Rooiribbok* **German:** *Bergriedbock* **French:** *Redunca de montagne*

Identification pointers Smaller of 2 reedbuck species in the region. Grey-fawn to reddish-brown upperparts with white underparts, including area below bushy tail. Hair on neck and head usually more yellow-fawn, and lower legs often paler than rest of upper body. Ears long and narrow, lined with white hairs on inner surface. Only ram carries short, stout, forward-curved and heavily ringed horns. Bare glandular patch below each ear.

Similar Common reedbuck larger and can be separated on habitat preferences. See also grey rhebok as ranges overlap considerably.

Habitat Mountainous and rocky slopes, but shows preference for broken hill country with scattered trees, bush clumps and open grassy slopes.

Behaviour May feed at night or during day. Can be very difficult to spot standing still on grassed slopes. Rams attempt to hold territories on year-round basis. Small groups of 2–6 ewes and their young move from herd to herd, crossing freely through ram territories, but may spend long periods within range of a single ram. Small bachelor groups also form, but are unstable.

Food Predominantly grasses, with some seasonal preferences.

Reproduction Single lamb, weighing about 3 kg, born after gestation of some 242 days. Lamb remains hidden for first 2–3 months. Young may be born at any time of year, but birth peaks evident during rains. Ewe has 2 pairs inguinal mammae.

Longevity Up to 12 years in the wild.

Calls Usually only alarm and territorial nasal whistles heard.

Occurrence Southeastern sector of region and a near-endemic in South Africa. Occurs in numerous conservation areas and on private land. Mountain Zebra, Greater Addo, Gariep, Kruger, uKhuhlamba, Marakele (South Africa).

MEASUREMENTS
Weight: 30 kg
Shoulder height: 72 cm
Total length: 1.3–1.5 m
Tail length: 20 cm
Record horn length: 25.4 cm

Right front

43 mm

Right back

45 mm

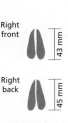

COMMON (SOUTHERN) REEDBUCK
Redunca arundinum

Afrikaans: *Rietbok* **German:** *Großer Riedbock* **French:** *Grand cobe des roseaux*

Identification pointers Medium-sized antelope; larger of 2 reedbuck species in the region. Uniform brown or greyish-fawn upperparts; head and neck usually slightly paler, but underparts and underside of bushy tail white. Usually has pale to white patch on upper throat. Vertical black, to dark brown, stripe on front of forelegs. Only ram carries fairly long, forward-curved horns, strongly ringed from base for about two-thirds of length. Base of horns narrowly ringed with pale grey growth tissue.

Similar Smaller mountain reedbuck has different habitat preferences. See also lechwe in Okavango area.

Habitat Occupies areas with tall grass and reed beds, close to permanent water. Avoids dense bush areas. From near sea level to about 2 000 m in South Africa.

Behaviour Most activity takes place at night, but in undisturbed areas may feed in cooler daylight hours. More nocturnal when food abundant, but diurnal feeding becomes prevalent during dry season. Does not form herd, but lives in pairs or small family parties. In areas of prime habitat, larger numbers may be seen feeding in close proximity. Territories defended by rams; conflicts involve elaborate and patterned displays.

Food Mainly grasses, but will also browse occasionally.

Reproduction Single fawn, weighing about 4.5 kg, born after 220-day gestation. Young are born any time of year. Fawn remains hidden for about first 2 months. After each suckling session (once or twice daily), fawn moves to new lying-up location. Ewe has 2 pairs inguinal mammae.

Longevity Up to 10 years in captivity; probably 6–8 years in the wild.

Calls Sharp, nasal whistle common.

Occurrence iSimangaliso, Kruger, uKhuhlamba, Marakele (South Africa); Chobe, Okavango/Moremi (Botswana); Hwange, Mana Pools, Gonarezhou (Zimbabwe); Caprivi (Namibia); Banhine, Gorongoza (Mozambique).

MEASUREMENTS
Weight: ♂ 43–68 kg; ♀ 32–51 kg
Shoulder height: ♂ 95 cm; ♀ 80 cm
Total length: ♂ 1.6–1.8 m; ♀ 1.4–1.7 m
Tail length: 25 cm
Record horn length: 46.68 cm

Right front — 65 mm

Right back — 61 mm

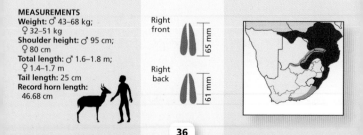

GREY RHEBOK

Pelea capreolus

Afrikaans: *Vaalribbok* **German:** *Rehantilope* **French:** *Pélén*

Identification pointers Gracefully built, with thick and woolly grey coat and white underparts. Well-haired tail with white underside, raised to show white when running away; runs with 'rocking-horse' motion. Ears long and narrow; large, black nose has swollen appearance. Only ram carries straight, smooth and upright horns.

Similar Shares habitat with mountain reedbuck. Klipspringer much smaller.

Habitat Usually in hilly or mountain country; also on adjacent flats, especially in Western Cape. From arid (Richtersveld) to high-rainfall (Drakensberg) areas, sea level to high altitudes.

Behaviour Predominantly diurnal, lying up at night. Normally in small family parties consisting of an adult territorial ram, several ewes and their young, to a maximum of 14 individuals. Young rams are chased away by territorial rams, disperse from family herd until old enough to establish and hold their own territory. Territory-holding ram is very aggressive and does not tolerate presence of other rams. In some areas is known to attack, and occasionally kill, mountain reedbuck rams.

Food Browse is important in most areas, but seems to vary between areas; will also graze, especially on fresh growth. Takes new grain seedlings in Western Cape.

Reproduction Single lamb born after gestation of about 260 days. Most births in September–January, with December–January peak. Lamb remains hidden at first. Ewe has 2 pairs inguinal mammae.

Longevity One captive > 12 years; probably averages 8 years in the wild.

Calls Sharp, nasal snort at regular intervals when disturbed or alarmed; also alarm 'cough'.

Occurrence Restricted to South Africa, Swaziland and Lesotho, with patchy distribution throughout. Isolated population in Huns Mountains, southwest Namibia. Richtersveld, Cedarberg, De Hoop, Agulhas, Karoo, Camdeboo, uKhahlamba (South Africa).

MEASUREMENTS
Weight: 20 kg
Shoulder height: 75 cm
Total length: 1.1–1.3 m
Tail length: 10 cm
Record horn length: 30.16 cm

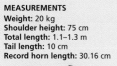

Right front

48 mm

Right back

45 mm

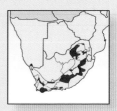

BLACK WILDEBEEST

Connochaetes gnou

Afrikaans: *Swartwildebees* **German:** *Weißschwanzgnu* **French:** *Gnou à queue blanche*

Identification pointers Shoulders higher than rump; head large and broad-snouted. Face covered in brush-like tuft of black hairs; long, black throat and neck mane, running on to chest. Dark brown, but may appear black from a distance. Mane of white, black-tipped hair on neck to upper shoulders. Horse-like tail white to dirty white, frequently swished from side to side, especially when running. Both sexes carry horns that bend steeply downward, forward and upward. Horns of cow lighter; forms boss in prime bull.

Similar Blue wildebeest is larger.

Habitat Low karroid scrub and open grassland.

Behaviour Diurnal, but on occasion may graze at night. Most feeding takes place during cooler daylight hours. Bulls establish territories and will attempt to 'herd' cows within their areas during rut. Nursery herds of cows and their young normally wander freely over bulls' territories. Bulls mark their territories using urine, droppings, scent secretions and elaborate displays, throughout the year. Bachelor herds consist of bulls of all ages. When running, tend to zigzag, changing direction and swishing prominent white tail.

Food Principally feeds on grasses, but also on low Karoo bushes, especially during dry season. Access to water essential.

Reproduction Single calf, weighing about 14 kg, born after gestation of some 250 days. Most births during mid-summer (December–January), but there is some area variation. Young can move with herd shortly after birth. Cow has 1 pair inguinal mammae.

Longevity One captive lived 19 years 7 months; probably less in the wild.

Calls Characteristic nasal call *ge-nu*; snorts.

Occurrence Central plains South African endemic; introduced widely on Namibian game farms. Was close to extinction, now numbers > 20 000. Camdeboo, Mountain Zebra, Golden Gate Highlands, Willem Pretorius (South Africa).

MEASUREMENTS
Weight: ♂ 180 kg;
♀ 100–140 kg
Shoulder height: ♂ 1.2 m; ♀ 1.1 m
Total length: 2.6–3.2 m
Tail length: 80–100 cm
Record horn length: 74.62 cm
(tip to tip along curves)

Right front

90 mm

Right back

83 mm

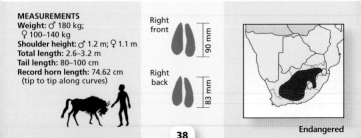

Endangered

BLUE WILDEBEEST

Connochaetes taurinus

Afrikaans: *Blouwildebees* **German:** *Streifengnu* **French:** *Gnou bleu*

Identification pointers Lightly built hindquarters, but more robust at shoulders and chest. Head large, with broad snout. Black facial blaze, mane and throat fringe. Both sexes carry black horns, which grow outwards, turn sharply up and then turn inwards; horn bases form a separated boss. Distinctive black, horse-like tail. Overall coat colour dark grey, tinged with brown, with several vertical, darker stripes on neck and chest.

Similar Black wildebeest smaller, with darker coat, black 'brush' of hair on face; different horn structure.

Habitat Prefers open savanna woodland and open grassland. Access to drinking water essential.

Behaviour Feeds during cooler daylight hours, but may feed at other times. Lives in herds of up to 30 individuals, but forms much larger groups at times, while maintaining herd integrity. Some populations resident, but others nomadic (Kgalagadi, Etosha), following rains and new grass growth. Territorial bulls defend zone around their cows, even when migrating. Territorial bull may control 2–150 cows; cows may wander through mobile territories of several bulls.

Food Short, green grass when available.

Reproduction. Single calf, weighing about 22 kg, born after gestation of about 250 days. Mating mainly March to June, with most births from mid-November to end-December, but this is variable. Cow has 1 pair inguinal mammae.

Longevity 20 years in captivity; 18 years in the wild.

Calls Characteristic metallic *gnou* grunt; snorts. Calf bleats.

Occurrence Natural range in north and northeast of region; widely introduced outside this. Hluhluwe-Imfolozi, uMkhuze, Ithala, Kruger, Madikwe, Pilanesberg, Mapungubwe, Kgalagadi (South Africa); Hwange, Gonarezhou (Zimbabwe); Central Kalahari, Chobe (Botswana); Khaudom, Etosha (Namibia).

MEASUREMENTS
Weight: ♂ 250 kg; ♀ 180 kg
Shoulder height: ♂ 1.5 m; ♀ 1.3 m
Total length: 2.4–3.3 m
Tail length: 45 cm–1 m
Record horn length: 86.05 cm (tip to tip along curves)

Right front

100 mm

Right back

100 mm

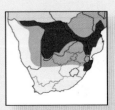

RED HARTEBEEST

Alcelaphus buselaphus

Afrikaans: *Rooihartbees* **German:** *Kuhantilope* **French:** *Bubale roux*

Identification pointers High shouldered, with back sloping down to rump. Long, pointed head with black blaze down front of face. Coat fawn to golden-brown overall, but darker from shoulders down centre of back to rump; rump and upper thighs paler. Large areas of black on legs. Tail black with pale base. Both sexes carry horns; bull's horns heavier, set close together at base, curving forwards and out, then twisting in and back.

Similar See Lichtenstein's hartebeest, but very limited range and no natural range overlap, no black blaze or black on legs. Tsessebe has widely spreading lyrate horns; minimal range overlap.

Habitat Open grassed savanna and open woodland. Can go without drinking water.

Behaviour Mostly diurnal. Congregates in herds of about 20 individuals, running to several hundred, rarely in thousands (Kalahari). Larger groups usually form at onset of summer rains. In larger arid areas will travel great distances in search of fresh growth. Adult bull is territorial. Adult bull and harem herd of cows and young occupy best grazing. Bachelor herds make do with areas on periphery of established territories.

Food Mainly grazes, but some browse included in diet; usually low shrubs and herbaceous plants.

Reproduction Single calf, weighing 12–14 kg, born after gestation of about 240 days. Most births October–December, coinciding with onset of summer rains. Calf born away from herd, remaining hidden until strong enough to keep up. Cow has 1 pair inguinal mammae.

Longevity 19 years in captivity; 10–12 years in the wild (often less).

Calls Sneeze-snort alarm call.

Occurrence Occurred over much of west-central area of region; in recent years widely reintroduced and occurs in good numbers. Etosha, Khaudom (Namibia); Kgalagadi, Pilanesberg, Madikwe, Greater Addo, Mountain Zebra (South Africa); Nxai Pan, Central Kalahari, Makgadikgadi (Botswana).

MEASUREMENTS
Weight: ♂ 150 kg; ♀ 120 kg
Shoulder height: 1.25 m
Total length: 2.3 m
Tail length: 47 cm
Record horn length: 74.93 cm

Right front

100 mm

Right back

96 mm

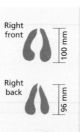

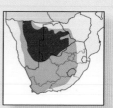

LICHTENSTEIN'S HARTEBEEST
Alcelaphus lichtensteini

Afrikaans: *Lichtenstein-hartbees* **German:** *Lichtenstein-Kuhantilope* **French:** *Bubale de Lichtenstein*

Identification pointers Typical hartebeest form, with shoulders higher than rump. Long, slender head and narrow, pointed ears. Overall body colour yellow-fawn to pale reddish-fawn, with a slightly darker 'saddle' stretching from shoulders to rump. Flanks, rump and lower legs lighter in colour. Tail black with pale base. Both sexes have horns flattened at the base, strongly ringed, except at tips, and with a 'Z'-shaped curvature.

Similar Does not overlap with red hartebeest. Tsessebe has black facial blaze and leg markings and different horn form.

Habitat Savanna woodland adjoining marsh areas and flood plains, with ready access to water.

Behaviour Feeds mainly by day, but nocturnal feeding not unusual. In small nursery herds of up to 10 individuals. Territorial bull stays in vicinity of his group of cows and their young within fixed home range, which usually has best grazing. Bachelor herds have to utilize less favourable feeding grounds. Hierarchy exists among females, with older cows dominant. Herd male marks territory with droppings at midden sites, urine, and secretions from facial glands.

Food Almost exclusively a grass eater.

Reproduction Single calf, weighing about 15 kg, born after gestation of 240 days. Calf may follow mother soon after birth, but lies out in the open between suckling sessions. Young are born June–September. Cow has 1 pair inguinal mammae.

Longevity No age known, but probably similar to red hartebeest.

Calls Frog-like quacks and grunts; alarm sneeze-snort. Not particularly vocal.

Occurrence Small natural population in Mozambique and southeast Zimbabwe (Gonarezhou) and reintroduced to Kruger (South Africa) from Malawi.

MEASUREMENTS
Weight: ♂ 160–204 kg;
♀ 160–180 kg
Shoulder height: 1.25 m
Total length: 2.01–2.5 m
Record horn length: 61.92 cm

Right front
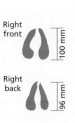
100 mm

Right back
96 mm

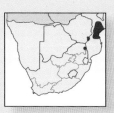

41

1 BONTEBOK
2 BLESBOK

Damaliscus pygargus dorcas
Damaliscus pygargus phillipsi

Afrikaans: *Bontebok, Blesbok* **German:** *Buntbock, Blessbock* **French:** *Bontebok, Blesbok*

Identification pointers Distinct subspecies of *Damaliscus pygargus*. Medium-sized, with shoulders higher than rump and long, pointed head. Both sexes carry simple lyre-shaped horns, those of ewes being more slender. Bontebok has rich, dark brown coat with purple gloss, especially ram; darker on sides and upper legs; white buttocks and lower limbs; usually an unbroken white facial blaze; horns all black. Blesbok has reddish-brown coat and no gloss; buttocks pale but not white; white blaze usually broken between eyes; horns straw-coloured on front ringed surface.

Similar Should not be confused with other species, but see much larger red hartebeest.

Habitat Bontebok: coastal plain of fynbos (heathland), with low scrub and grass. Blesbok: open grassland with access to water.

Behaviour Diurnal. Territorial bontebok rams hold their areas throughout year and ewe/lamb groups numbering 6–10 wander at will through adjoining territories. Ewe groups herded January to March in rut. Bachelor groups circulate beyond territories. Blesbok ewes roam in harem herds of 2–25, each herd attended by territorial ram.

Food Grasses, occasionally takes browse.

Reproduction Single lamb, weighing 6–7 kg, born after gestation of about 240 days. Bontebok lambs born September–October; most blesbok lambs November–January. Can run with mother about 30 minutes after birth. Ewe has 1 pair inguinal mammae.

Longevity Bontebok up to 15 years in captivity; blesbok up to 21 years in captivity; probably much less in the wild.

Calls Snorts of alarm; sneeze vocalisation.

Occurrence Introduced to Namibia and in South Africa outside range. **Bontebok:** Table Mountain, Agulhas, De Hoop, Bontebok. **Blesbok:** Willem Pretorius, Mountain Zebra (South Africa).

MEASUREMENTS
Weight: Bontebok ♂ 62 kg;
Blesbok ♂ 70 kg
(in both cases ♀ lighter)
Shoulder height:
Bontebok 90 cm; Blesbok 95 cm
Total length: 1.7–2.0 m
Tail length: 30–45 cm
Record horn length:
Bontebok 43 cm;
Blesbok 52.39 cm

Right front
62 mm

Right back
63 mm

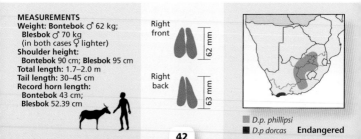

D.p. phillipsi
D.p dorcas **Endangered**

TSESSEBE

Damaliscus lunatus

Afrikaans: *Tsessebe* **German:** *Leierantilope* **French:** *Sassaby*, *Damalisque*

Identification pointers Hartebeest-like in appearance, with shoulders higher than rump and long face. Upperparts dark reddish-brown with distinct purplish sheen, especially in bull. Head, lower shoulder and upperparts of legs darker in colour than rest of body. Lower parts of legs brownish-yellow, with pale fawn inner thighs. Tail pale fawn at base, black tassel on terminal half. Both sexes carry widespread lyrate horns, ringed except at tip.

Similar Compare with red hartebeest and Lichtenstein's hartebeest, but range overlap minimal and horn forms differ.

Habitat Open savanna woodland with adjacent grassland and access to surface water.

Behaviour Mainly diurnal, but some nocturnal activity. Forms small herds of 5–6 individuals, but sometimes as many as 30 in the region, especially at favourable feeding sites or close to water. Territorial bull maintains a defended area, within which cows and young animals live permanently. Groups of young males form fluid bachelor herds that circulate around perimeter of established territories, usually with access to less favourable grazing. Territory-holding bulls mark their territory with dropping heaps and secretions from facial glands.

Food Exclusive grass eaters, mainly medium to taller grasses.

Reproduction Single lamb, weighing 10–12 kg, born after gestation of about 240 days. Birth peaks October–December at onset of rains. Calves can run with herd a short time after birth. Cow has 1 pair inguinal mammae.

Longevity A captive lived > 9 years; an estimate of 15 years in the wild.

Calls Frog-like quacks and grunts; snorts.

Occurrence Patchy distribution in north and northeast. Mokala, Pilanesberg, Madikwe, Marakele, Kruger (South Africa); Chobe (Botswana); Caprivi (Namibia); Hwange (Zimbabwe).

MEASUREMENTS
Weight: ♂ 140 kg; ♀ 126 kg
Shoulder height: 1.2 m
Total length: 1.9–2.3 m
Tail length: 45 cm
Record horn length: 46.99 cm

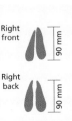

Right front — 90 mm

Right back — 90 mm

IMPALA

Aepyceros melampus

Afrikaans: *Rooibok* **German:** *Impala, Schwarzfersenantilope* **French:** *Impala*

Identification pointers Medium-sized antelope, lightly built and graceful, with reddish-fawn upperparts becoming paler on sides. White chest, belly, throat and chin. Tail is white with central black line on upper surface and each buttock has vertical, black blaze. Only antelope with tuft of black hair on lower rear-edge of back leg. Ram carries long, graceful lyrate horns, deeply ringed for much of their length. Black-faced impala (*A.m. petersi*) of northern Namibia has dark blaze down front of face and more bushy tail.

Similar Compare with puku in northern Botswana and springbok (horns differ).

Habitat Open or light savanna woodland; avoids open grassland unless adjoining bush cover.

Behaviour Active mainly during cooler daylight hours, but also feeds at night. Nursery herds of ewes and young may overlap with seasonal territories of several rams. During breeding season (tied closely to onset of rains), territorial ram separates out 15–20 ewes for mating. Bachelor herds tend to occupy areas away from breeding herds. Outside rut, rams live in bachelor herds and nursery herds re-form.

Food True mixed feeder; both grasses and browse eaten.

Reproduction Single lamb, weighing about 5 kg, born after gestation of 196 days average. Ewe has 2 pairs inguinal mammae.

Longevity 15 years in captivity; 12 years in the wild.

Calls Ram very vocal during the rut, with repertoire of growls, roars and snorts. Ewe and lamb communicate with soft bleat.

Occurrence One of most common antelope in northeast of region. Widely introduced outside natural range. Black-faced impala only naturally occurs in northwest Namibia, and in much lower numbers. Etosha (Namibia); Chobe, Nxai Pan (Botswana); Hwange, Mana Pools, Gonarezhou (Zimbabwe); Pilanesberg, Madikwe, Marakele, Mapungubwe, Kruger, uMkhuze, Hluhluwe-Imfolozi (South Africa).

MEASUREMENTS
Weight: ♂ 45–80 kg (average 50 kg);
♀ 34–52 kg (average 40 kg)
Shoulder height: 90 cm
Total length: 1.6–1.72 m
Tail length: 28 cm
Record horn length: 78.4 cm (impala); 67.9 cm (black-faced impala)

Right front

47 mm

Right back

46 mm

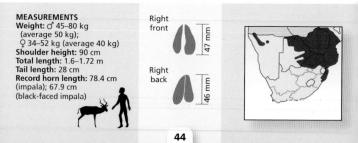

SPRINGBOK

Antidorcas marsupialis

Afrikaans: *Springbok* **German:** *Springbock* **French:** *Springbok*

Identification pointers Hindquarters slightly higher than shoulders and distinctively marked. Dark red-brown band along flanks separates fawn-brown upperparts from white underparts. Head white with brown stripe running through eye to corner of upper lip. Large white patch on rump bordered with brown stripe. Long-haired, white erectile crest from mid-back to rump normally covered, but raised when 'pronking' (stiff-legged jumping). Both sexes carry heavily ridged, lyre-shaped horns, but rams heavier and longer. Two races, the Karoo (*A.m. marsupialis*) and Kalahari (*A.m. hofmeyeri*); latter is larger.
Similar See impala, but more reddish-brown, with black buttock lines; horns differ.
Habitat Open, arid plains; avoids dense cover. Access to water not essential.
Behaviour Active during cooler daylight hours, but forages to a certain extent at night. Small herds, but when moving to new feeding grounds may congregate in hundreds, sometimes thousands (Kalahari).

Small herds mixed or rams only; solitary rams often seen. Rams territorial, and will herd ewe groups during the rut, but do not hold territories through the year. Territory-holding rams have elaborate displays to intimidate potential rivals.
Food Grass and browse; will dig for roots and bulbs with front hooves.
Reproduction Single lamb, weighing about 3.8 kg, born after gestation of about 168 days. Births any time, but commonly coincide with rains. Lamb joins herd with mother after about 2 days. Ewe has 1 pair (rarely 2) inguinal mammae.
Longevity Up to 19 years in captivity; probably 7–10 in the wild.
Calls Low grumbling-grunt among herd members; sharp whistle when alarmed; lamb bleats.
Occurrence Main populations in Etosha, Namib-Naukluft (Namibia); Kgalagadi, Karoo, Mountain Zebra (South Africa); Central Kalahari, Makgadikgadi, Nxai Pan (Botswana).

MEASUREMENTS
Weight: ♂ 32–46 kg
♀ 26–38 kg
Shoulder height: 75 cm
Total length: 1.12–1.27 m
Tail length: 25 cm
Record horn length: 49.22 cm

Right front

55 mm

Right back

54 mm

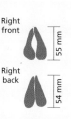

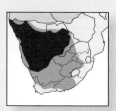

DAMARA DIK-DIK

Madoqua damarensis

Afrikaans: *Damara-dikdik* **German:** *Damaradikdik* **French:** *Dik-dik de Damara*

Identification pointers Tiny antelope characterized by elongated, very mobile nose; large, white-ringed eyes. Upperparts yellowish-grey with grizzled appearance; neck paler than shoulders and flanks. Underparts white to off-white, with white to pale patch on upper throat. Tuft of long hair on forehead is erected when animal is alarmed, or in conflict with rivals. Ram has short, spike-like horns that slope back at angle of facial profile, may be partially hidden by crest.

Similar Steenbok is similar but larger, with uniform red-brown upperparts. Steenbok rams have smooth, erect horns.

Habitat Fairly dense, dry woodland. Penetrates Namib Desert along wooded watercourses. Bush-covered hillsides and adjacent scrub may be occupied.

Behaviour Diurnal and nocturnal. Usually solitary or in pairs, but also small family parties, which may include up to 2 adult females. Pairs live within small home range and are territorial, with both rams and ewe defending the territory; ram chases away other rams and ewe sees off intruding ewes. Communal dung middens are established, and twigs are marked with secretions from a gland in front of the eye. Uses same pathways between resting and feeding sites in territory.

Food Predominantly browses leaves, flowers, fruit and seed pods. Takes some fresh grass growth when available. Will scratch for roots with front hooves.

Reproduction Single fawn, weighing 620–760 g, born after gestation of about 170 days. Most births in wet season (January–March). Ewe has 2 pairs inguinal mammae.

Longevity More than 15–16 years in captivity; probably < 5 years in the wild.

Calls Sharp alarm whistle; lower key whistle seems to be communication between individuals; authors have heard twittering contact call.

Occurrence Skeleton Coast, Etosha, Waterberg, Khaudom (Namibia).

MEASUREMENTS
Weight: 5 kg (average)
Shoulder height: 38 cm
Total length: 64–76 cm
Tail length: 5 cm
Record horn length: 10.48 cm (Namibia)

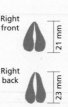

Right front — 21 mm

Right back — 23 mm

SUNI

Neotragus moschatus

Afrikaans: *Soenie* **German:** *Moschusböckchen, Suni* **French:** *Suni*

Identification pointers Tiny, elegant dwarf antelope with rich rufous-brown upperparts flecked with white hairs. Underparts white to off-white. Has 2 slightly curved white bars on throat, and above each hoof a narrow, dark band. Tail is dark brown above, has white tip and is flicked regularly and rapidly. Only ram carries short, thick, prominently ridged horns that slope backwards in line with face. Rather transparent, pink-lined ears.
Similar Sharpe's grysbok is larger, with more white flecking on coat and very short tail; ram's horns are smooth. Similar-sized blue duiker has uniform grey coat. See also larger red duiker.
Habitat Dry thickets and riverine woodland with dense undergrowth.
Behaviour Mainly nocturnal, but also during cooler hours of daylight. Usually lives in pairs, or small groups of 1 adult ram and up to 4 ewes with associated young. Ram is territorial, marking areas with glandular deposits and dung heaps.

When disturbed, runs off in zigzag pattern, similar to that of startled hare. Makes regular use of the same pathways, making them very vulnerable to snaring.
Food Browse most important; feeds on a wide range of plant species.
Reproduction Single young, weighing about 750 g, born after gestation of about 180 days. Births may occur at any time of year. Fawn remains hidden for first few weeks of life, only emerging to suckle. Ewe has 2 pairs inguinal mammae.
Longevity 9 years on record in captivity; probably less in the wild.
Calls Wheezing-screech when alarmed; *chee-chee* sneezing-whistle; frequent quiet snorts.
Occurrence Widespread and common in Mozambique; only marginal in rest of far east of region. Largest populations in South Africa: Thembe Elephant Reserve (> 3 000), Phinda Resource Reserve (> 500), False Bay Park (± 350); others include Ndumo, uMkhuze, Kruger.

MEASUREMENTS
Weight: 5.1–6.8 kg
(♂ averages heavier than ♀)
Shoulder height: 35 cm
Total length: 68–75 cm
Tail length: 12 cm
Record horn length:
13.3 cm

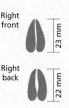

Right front

Right back

23 mm

22 mm

KLIPSPRINGER

Oreotragus oreotragus

Afrikaans: *Klipspringer* **German:** *Klippspringer* **French:** *Oréotrague*

Identification pointers Small, stocky antelope, with very short tail, coarse, spiny hair usually yellow-brown to grey-brown, and overall grizzled appearance. Paler underparts, generally grey-white to brownish-white. Ears rounded, broad and bordered with black, but inner hairs white. Ram carries short horns, widely separated at base, vertical and only ringed close to head. Walks on tips of hooves.

Similar Habitat should separate it from any other species, but see much larger grey rhebok. Sharpe's grysbok in northeast and Cape grysbok in southwest are both redder in colour, rarely on open, rocky terrain.

Habitat Rugged, rocky areas from coastal hills, isolated outcrops and highest mountain ranges, such as Drakensberg.

Behaviour Most active during cooler daylight hours, or throughout the day when overcast or cool. Lives in pairs or small family parties. Ram is strongly territorial. Communal dung middens scattered through home range; both sexes mark twigs with secretions from glands in front of eyes. Choice of home range dependent on food quality and abundance, varies in size from 8–49 ha. Agile, even in very rugged, rocky terrain.

Food Predominantly browses, but eats green grass when available.

Reproduction Single lamb, weighing about 1 kg, born after gestation of about 210 days. Young born any time of year. Lamb remains hidden for first 1–3 months of life. Ewe has 2 pairs inguinal mammae.

Longevity 15 years in captivity; probably 6–8 years in the wild.

Calls Loud nasal whistle, snorts.

Occurrence Occurs in many parks and reserves where there is suitable habitat. Etosha, Namib-Naukluft, Fish River (Namibia); Richtersveld, Augrabies, Namaqua, Cedarberg, Table Mountain, De Hoop, Garden Route, uMkhahlamba, Hluhluwe-Imfolozi, Kruger, Madikwe, Pilanesberg, Mapungubwe (South Africa); Matobo, Hwange, Mana Pools (Zimbabwe).

MEASUREMENTS
Weight: ♂ 10 kg; ♀ 13 kg
Shoulder height: 50–60 cm
Total length: 80 cm–1 m
Tail length: 8 cm
Record horn length: 16.19 cm

Right front

21 mm

Right back

20 mm

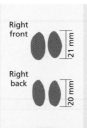

STEENBOK

Raphicerus campestris

Afrikaans: *Steenbok* **German:** *Steinböckchen* **French:** *Steenbok*

Identification pointers Small, elegant dwarf antelope with large, white-ringed eyes and very large ears. Upperparts normally rufous-fawn to deeper chestnut, with white underparts. Pale fawn to white patch usually present on upper throat. Very short tail a uniform rufous-fawn. Only ram carries short, sharp-pointed, smooth-surfaced horns that rise near-vertically from head. Although 5 subspecies are listed for the region, most are suspect.

Similar See oribi, which is larger, with black-tipped tail and smaller ears. Grysbok has longer, white-flecked coat.

Habitat Open country with some cover; will penetrate very arid areas along dry riverbeds. Drinking water not essential.

Behaviour Lies up in cover during heat of day, feeding during cooler hours. Nocturnal feeding also common, especially in areas where regularly hunted or disturbed. Solitary, ram/ewe pairs, or mother with young. Both sexes are strongly defensive of jointly held territories. Unlike other antelope, defecates and urinates in shallow scrape dug with front hooves, then covers it. Can reach high densities in optimal habitat.

Food Mixed feeder, taking grasses, browse, seed pods and fruit. During dry times digs out roots and bulbs with front hooves.

Reproduction A single lamb, weighing about 900 g, born after gestation of some 170 days. Lamb remains hidden for several weeks to 3 months after birth. Births any time of year, with possible summer peaks in some areas. Ewe has 2 pairs inguinal mammae.

Longevity 10–12 years in captivity; usually less in the wild.

Calls Alarm snorts; soft bleating, especially between mother and lamb.

Occurrence Very wide range in the region, wherever there is suitable habitat, even thriving in many farming areas. Occurs in virtually all conservation areas.

MEASUREMENTS
Weight: 9–13 kg
Shoulder height: 50 cm
Total length: 75–90 cm
Tail length: 5 cm
Record horn length: 19.05 cm

Right front

39 mm

Right back

40 mm

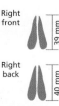

♀ ♂

ORIBI

Ourebia ourebi

Afrikaans: *Oorbietjie* **German:** *Oribi* **French:** *Ourébi*

Identification pointers Largest of the dwarf antelope, with rufous yellow-orange upperparts and white underparts and inner thighs. Neck relatively long and slender, ears medium-sized. Short tail has prominent black tip. Hair on back often has curly appearance. Only ram carries short, erect and partly ringed horns. Dark marking gland visible below ear. Although 3 subspecies have been described from the region, these are based on minor colour variations; all can be identified as oribi.

Similar Steenbok smaller, smooth-coated, with very short reddish-brown tail and large ears; limited range overlap.

Habitat Open, short grassland with taller grass patches for cover.

Behaviour Mainly diurnal. Occurs in pairs or small parties with 1 adult ram and up to 4 ewes. Ram is vigorously territorial and marks grass stalks with facial gland secretions; droppings deposited in communal dung heaps. Very bound to home range and rarely leaves it, even

when under stress. When disturbed, runs rapidly, with occasional pronks (stiff-legged jumps), clearly displaying black-tipped tail; after covering a short distance, will usually stop and turn towards threat.

Food Principally a grazer, but browse sometimes taken. Marked preference for short grasses; will move to another part of range if grass gets too long.

Reproduction Single lamb, weighing 1.8 kg average, born after gestation of about 210 days. Births throughout year, with distinct peak during rains. Lamb remains hidden in long grass for first 3–4 months. Ewe has 2 pairs inguinal mammae.

Longevity Up to 14 years in captivity.

Calls Sharp whistle or sneeze when alarmed.

Occurrence. In KwaZulu-Natal Drakensberg (uKhahlamba) and Midlands perhaps 3 000 survive; fewer than 500 in Eastern Cape. Chobe (Botswana); Gonarezhou (Zimbabwe); uKhahlamba, Ithala (South Africa).

MEASUREMENTS
Weight: 14–20 kg (♂ averages 2 kg lighter than ♀)
Shoulder height: 60 cm
Total length: 1.1 m
Tail length: 6–15 cm
Record horn length: 19.05 cm

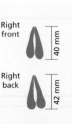

Right front

40 mm

Right back

42 mm

Endangered (SA)

CAPE GRYSBOK

Raphicerus melanotis

Afrikaans: *Kaapse grysbok* **German:** *Kap-Greisbock* **French:** *Grysbok, Raphicère du Cap*

Identification pointers Small, squat antelope with rufous-brown upperparts abundantly flecked with white hairs. Flanks and neck have fewer white hairs; underparts lighter than upperparts. Grey-brown ears proportionately large with white hairs on inner surface. Tail very short. Only ram has short, smooth, slightly back-angled horns.

Similar Sharpe's grysbok, but ranges do not overlap. Steenbok lacks white flecking on coat, occurs in open habitat.

Habitat Occupies areas with relatively thick scrub-bush, almost entirely within fynbos (heathland) vegetation, including scrub-covered sand dunes, wooded gorges on mountain slopes, riverine scrub and low, bush-covered hillsides. Frequently found on fringes of agricultural land where belts of natural vegetation survive.

Behaviour Mainly nocturnal and very secretive, but also active in early morning and late afternoon hours if not disturbed; also active on cool, overcast days. Usually solitary, except when mating, or when ewe tending lamb. Home range size largely dictated by season and food availability. Male is strongly territorial. Ranges of males are small, measuring 1–9 ha, and do not overlap; ranges of females do overlap. Although a hierarchical system seems to be in play, this has not been confirmed. Territories are marked with large dung heaps and secretions from preorbital glands.

Food Mainly browses but takes some grass. Disliked in vineyards as it eats young grape clusters and terminal buds.

Reproduction Single lamb, weighing about 850 g, born after gestation of about 180 days. Birth peaks in spring and summer. Ewe has 2 pairs inguinal mammae.

Longevity A captive lived 7 years.

Calls Soft bleat between ewe and lamb; low alarm sneeze.

Occurrence Restricted range but fairly common. Namaqua, Cedarberg, West Coast, Table Mountain, Agulhas, De Hoop, Garden Route, Greater Addo (South Africa).

MEASUREMENTS
Weight: 10 kg
Shoulder height: 54 cm
Total length: 72–81 cm
Tail length: 5.5 cm
Record horn length: 13.34 cm (South Africa)

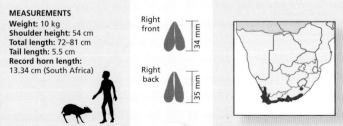

Right front — 34 mm
Right back — 35 mm

SHARPE'S GRYSBOK

Raphicerus sharpei

Afrikaans: *Sharpe-grysbok* **German:** *Sharpe-Greisbock* **French:** *Grysbok de Sharpe*

Identification pointers Small and stockily built. Reddish-brown upperparts liberally flecked with white hairs, giving grizzled appearance; fewer to no white hairs on head, neck and legs. Underparts buff to buffy-white, but never pure white. Tail very short and same colour as upper body. Fairly short in leg. Only ram carries short, sharp-pointed, smooth, slightly back-angled horns.

Similar Steenbok lacks white hair flecking and occupies open terrain. See also suni, but this has less flecking and longish tail; ram has heavily ringed, strongly back-angled horns. Blue duiker smaller, uniformly coloured and has more prominent tail.

Habitat Requires areas with relatively dense vegetation cover, especially low thicket with adjacent open grassed glades. Commonly associated with vegetated rocky hills and in scrub at their base.

Behaviour Although mainly nocturnal, quite often seen during cooler daylight hours and on overcast days. Normally solitary, but usually a pair lives in loose association within same home range. Ram believed to be territorial, but little studied. Territories are marked with large dung middens; secretions from black, bare gland in front of eye are rubbed onto tips of twigs and plant stalks.

Food Mostly browses, taking leaves, pods, fruit and berries, but also eats some grass and will dig for roots and bulbs with front hooves.

Reproduction Single lamb, weighing about 900 g born after estimated 200-day gestation. Births any time of year, although may peak with rains. Ewe has 2 pairs inguinal mammae.

Longevity Not known, but probably to at least 10 years.

Calls Quiet bleat, rarely heard.

Occurrence Restricted to northeast of region; not uncommon in parts of Zimbabwe and Mozambique. Mana Pools, Gonarezhou (Zimbabwe); Mapungubwe, Kruger (South Africa).

MEASUREMENTS
Weight: 7.5 kg
Shoulder height: 50 cm
Total length: 65–80 cm
Tail length: 6 cm
Record horn length: 6.35 cm

Right front
25 mm

Right back
25 mm

RED DUIKER
Cephalophus natalensis

Afrikaans: *Rooiduiker* **German:** *Rotducker* **French:** *Céphalophe du Natal*

Identification pointers Small, thickset antelope with relatively short legs; gives back arched appearance. Overall body colour is rich reddish-brown to deep chestnut, with marginally lighter underparts. Tail is tipped in black and white. Both sexes carry short, sharp, back-sloping horns. Longish crest on top of head, may obscure horns. Two subspecies sometimes recognized based on minor coloration differences, but both similar.

Similar Blue duiker much smaller, with uniform bluish-grey coat. Sharpe's grysbok and suni both smaller, with sprinkling of white hairs.

Habitat Most forest types and associated thickets, including on mountain slopes and in lowlands.

Behaviour Diurnal, lying up under cover at night. Usually solitary animals seen, but pairs may live in loose association in same home range. Can reach quite high densities in some areas. Droppings are deposited in small heaps in specific areas that, along with glandular secretions, demarcate territory. Often feeds on dropped items under trees where monkeys and baboons are feeding.

Food Wide range of plant food, including leaves, flowers, fruit and seeds. Opens hard monkey orange fruit by stabbing them with the horns against a rock or log. Like most duikers, also eats some animal food (insects, birds, small mammals).

Reproduction Single fawn, weighing < 1 kg, born after gestation estimated at 210 days, but likely less than 200 days. Young probably born any time of year. Ewe has 2 pairs inguinal mammae.

Longevity A captive lived to 6 years, but an unconfirmed report gives 12 years.

Calls Whistles and soft snorts.

Occurrence Limited to far east of region, with an isolated western population in the Soutpansberg range, South Africa's Limpopo province. iSimangaliso, uMkhuze, Hluhluwe-Imfolozi, Kruger (South Africa); Banhine, Gorongoza (Mozambique).

MEASUREMENTS
Weight: 10–16 kg
Shoulder height: 45 cm
Total length: 80 cm–1.1 m
Tail length: 9–15 cm
Record horn length:
10.48 cm (East Africa)

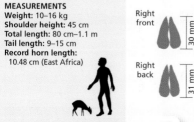

Right front

30 mm

Right back

31 mm

BLUE DUIKER

Cephalophus monticola

Afrikaans: *Blouduiker* **German:** *Blauducker* **French:** *Céphalophe bleu*

Identification pointers The smallest duiker, with delicate appearance; back arched. Overall body colour variable, from pale slate-grey to dark brown; on this basis some 3 subspecies are recognized from the region. However, similar variation exists within any single population. Legs typically a shade of brown, or brown-grey, usually contrasting with body. Throat and chest often paler. Both sexes carry short, sharp horns, but often hidden by crest of hair on top of head. Tail dark above and white below.
Similar Red duiker larger, different colour. Suni and Sharpe's grysbok flecked with white.

Habitat Wide range of forest and wooded habitats, including coastal dune forest and thicket, riverine and montane forest.
Behaviour Said to be strictly diurnal, with most activity in cooler morning and late afternoon hours. However, in areas of high disturbance will forage at night. Usually seen singly, but mated pairs occupy small,

permanent territories. Territory marked with secretions from gland in front of eye, tree-horning and piles of tiny droppings. Regularly uses same pathways between resting and feeding sites, making it very vulnerable to snaring.
Food Primarily a browser, taking a mix of wild fruit, berries, fresh and fallen leaves, fungi; some animal food, mainly insects.
Reproduction Single young, weighing about 400 g, born after gestation of estimated 200 days; some records give this as closer to 165 days. Young born any time of year, but with possible peaks. Ewe has 2 pairs of inguinal mammae.
Longevity Not known, but estimated 7–10 years.
Calls Whistles, snorts and hoof stamping.
Occurrence Restricted to narrow southern coastal belt and widely separated population in central Mozambique. Garden Route, Greater Addo, Oribi Gorge, iSimangaliso (South Africa).

MEASUREMENTS
Weight: 3.5–6 kg
Shoulder height: 35 cm
Total length: 62–84 cm
Tail length: 7–12 cm
Record horn length:
 7.3 cm (East Africa)

Right front
24 mm

Right back
22 mm

COMMON (GREY) DUIKER

Sylvicapra grimmia

Afrikaans: *Gewone duiker* **German:** *Kronenducker* **French:** *Céphalophe de Grimm*

Identification pointers Small antelope; walks and stands with straight back, not arched as in other 2 duiker species. Face has pinched appearance; crest of longish hair on top of head and usually a black facial blaze. As many as 6 subspecies have been described based on coat colour variations, but it is unlikely all are valid. Most coat coloration falls within light grey to reddish-brown to dark brown. Underparts may be marginally paler to white. Front of legs usually darker. Ram carries well-ringed, sharp-pointed, back-sloping horns.

Similar Red and blue duikers walk with arched backs and rarely share habitats with common. Sharpe's grysbok shorter in leg and smaller, with white-speckled coat.

Habitat Wide habitat tolerance, but mainly savanna woodland, thickets and open bush country.

Behaviour Most active at night, but frequently feeds during cooler daylight hours. Normally solitary, but pairs commonly seen. In areas of high density several individuals may feed in close proximity. Ram holds and marks territory, within which there is usually 1 ewe. Ram drives away other rams; female chases away other ewes. Measured home ranges extend from 6 ha to 27 ha.

Food Very wide range of plants, especially browse; seeks out and eats animal food such as termites, locusts and chicks of ground-nesting birds.

Reproduction Single lamb, weighing about 1.6 kg, born after gestation of some 190 days. Young born any time of year, but peaks coincide with rains. Ewe has 2 pairs inguinal mammae.

Longevity Almost 12 years in captivity; probably 6–8 years in the wild.

Calls Normally silent, but alarm bleats and snorts softly. If handled, gives blood-curdling scream.

Occurrence Occurs across much of region; absent only from Namib Desert and a few areas with unsuitable habitat. Present in most conservation areas.

MEASUREMENTS
Weight: ♂ 18 kg; ♀ 21 kg
Shoulder height: 50 cm
Total length: 90–135 cm
Tail length: 10–22 cm
Record horn length: 18.1 cm

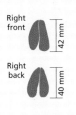

Right front 42 mm

Right back 40 mm

SAVANNA (AFRICAN) ELEPHANT
Loxodonta africana

Afrikaans: *Olifant* **German:** *Afrikanischer Elefant* **French:** *Éléphant de savane d'Afrique*

Identification pointers Unmistakable, with vast size, long trunk, large ears and tusks. Tusks usually carried by both sexes, but some animals lack tusks. Grey-brown skin usually hairless; takes on colour of local soil from mud- and dust-bathing.

Similar Cannot be mistaken.

Habitat Wide habitat tolerance, including coastal regions, lowland and montane forest, different savanna associations, swamp, semi-desert and desert. Desert generally accessed along watercourses, but will cross sand dunes.

Behaviour Diurnal and nocturnal. Matriarchal or family groups usually occupy home ranges of 15 km² to > 50 km², but mature bull may cover much larger area. Small family herds consist of an older cow (the matriarch) and offspring, with larger groups of related cows and calves. Herds numbering in the hundreds may gather, but are usually temporary, and matriarchal herds maintain their integrity. Bull often solitary, or in small, loose grouping, circulating matriarchal herds, testing cows for readiness to mate. Complex means of communication, including visual signs, touch, and audible, as well as sonic, calls.

Food Very wide variety of plants and plant parts, including browse and grass. In some areas high elephant densities have resulted in considerable damage to woodland trees (e.g. Chobe; Kruger). Seasonal preferences for certain plant foods.

Reproduction Single calf, weighing about 120 kg, born after 22-month gestation. Births can occur at any time of year. Cow has 1 pair pectoral mammae.

Longevity Up to 60 years in the wild.

Calls Rumbles, trumpeting, juvenile distress squeals, screams.

Occurrence Skeleton Coast, Etosha, Khaudom, Caprivi (Namibia); Chobe, Okavango, Moremi (Botswana); Hwange, Mana Pools, Gonarezhou (Zimbabwe); Mapungubwe, Kruger, Hluhluwe-Imfolozi, Madikwe, Pilanesberg, uMkhuze, Thembe, Greater Addo (South Africa).

MEASUREMENTS
Weight: ♂ 5 000–6 500 kg; ♀ 2 800–3 500 kg
Shoulder height: ♂ 3.2–4 m; ♀ 2.5–3.4 m
Total length: ♂ 7–9 m; ♀ 6.5–8.5 m
Tail length: 1.5 m
Heaviest tusks on record: 1 bull 102.3 kg, 97 kg (Kenya)

Right front — 500 mm
Right back — 520 mm

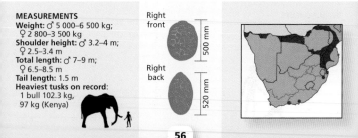

56

CARNIVORES

CAPE FOX

Vulpes chama

Afrikaans: *Silwervos* **German:** *Kapfuchs* **French:** *Renard du Cap*

Identification pointers Only 'true' fox in the region. Small, with slender build and large, pointed ears; seems quite long in leg. Overall colour of upperparts grizzled silvery-grey; lower limbs, face and backs of ears pale tawny-brown to reddish-brown. Inside ear lined with white hairs. Bushy tail is dark-tipped, 'pencilled' with dark brown to black, and appears darker than rest of coat. Underparts off-white to very pale fawn.

Similar Bat-eared fox darker, with black legs and larger ears. Black-backed jackal much larger and distinctly marked.

Habitat Open areas, such as grassland and arid scrub with low vegetation growth. Also extends into heathland (fynbos) in southwest, agricultural land and Namib Desert.

Behaviour Mainly nocturnal, but in areas of least disturbance may be active at dusk and dawn. Forms pairs, but male and female forage and hunt alone. Although several individuals have been

recorded sharing a den site, it is likely these consisted of a pair and well-grown young prior to dispersal. Dens are located in burrows excavated by other species, among dense vegetation and in crevices and rock scree. Home range size variable, but usually 1–4.6 km². Pups begin to forage on their own from 16th week, but remain with mother until 5th month.

Food Small rodents, young hares, invertebrates, reptiles, birds and some wild fruit; also scavenges. Very rarely will kill newborn sheep lambs.

Reproduction Litter of 1–5 (average 3) pups, born after gestation of 50–52 days. Young born in spring–summer (August–November). Female has 1 pair inguinal, 2 pairs abdominal mammae.

Longevity Probably 6–9 years, but information lacking.

Calls Sharp barking-yip; high-pitched, repeated yowl.

Occurrence Near-endemic to region. In virtually all conservation areas in range.

MEASUREMENTS
Weight: 2.5–4 kg
Shoulder height: 30–36 cm
Total length: 86–97 cm
Tail length: 23–34 cm

Right front

40 mm without claws

Right back
36 mm without claws

57

BAT-EARED FOX

Otocyon megalotis

Afrikaans: *Bakoorjakkals* **German:** *Löffelhund, Löffelfuchs*
French: *Otocyon, Renard à oreilles de chauve-souris*

Identification pointers Small, jackal-like canid with longish, slender legs and fairly long, sharp-pointed muzzle. Ears very large (14 cm), dark to black on back surface and lined with fringe of white hair on inside. Body covered in fairly long, silvery-grey hair with grizzled appearance, may have brownish tinge; lower legs usually dark to black. Face has silvery-white and black 'mask'. Bushy tail black above and at tip.
Similar See much lighter Cape fox, lacks face 'mask'. Two jackals in the region larger, with distinct body markings.
Habitat Open savanna country, savanna with short scrub, grassland, lightly wooded areas and semi-desert.
Behaviour Nocturnal and diurnal, largely depending on disturbance levels, also influenced by season in some areas. Retreats to shade during hottest hours. Capable of digging own burrow, but usually takes over and modifies one dug by other species. Typically seen running in groups of 2–6

individuals, consisting of a pair that mate for life and their offspring of the season. When foraging, appears to wander aimlessly, stopping periodically with ears to ground listening for underground prey movement.
Food Mainly insects, especially harvester termites, and numbers of small vertebrates. Wild berries, such as those of wild olive, spoonbush and crossberry, eaten at times.
Reproduction Litter of 1–6 (usually 2–4) pups, weighing 100–150 g, born after gestation of 60–75 days. Most births in the region from September to November. Female has 2 pairs inguinal mammae.
Longevity 13 years in captivity; probably much less in the wild.
Calls Several calls seldom heard; chirping from cub in distress; growl/ snarl combination; high-pitched bark.
Occurrence Very wide range across the region but absent from much of south and east coastal plains.

MEASUREMENTS
Weight: 3–5 kg
Shoulder height: 30–40 cm
Total length: 75–90 cm
Tail length: 23–34 cm

Right
front

36 mm
without claws

Right
back

39 mm
without claws

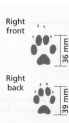

BLACK-BACKED JACKAL

Canis mesomelas

Afrikaans: *Rooijakkals* **German:** *Schabrackenschakal* **French:** *Chacal à chabraque*

Identification pointers Medium-sized, dog-like, with characteristic black saddle that is broad across the shoulders, narrows towards the tail base and is liberally sprinkled with white hairs. Face, flanks and legs pale to rich reddish-brown. Lips, throat and chest usually white (sometimes also underparts). Ears fairly large, pointed and reddish on back surface. Tail blackish; paler towards base.

Similar Side-striped jackal has white lateral stripe, shorter ears and white-tipped tail. Larger and differently marked than Cape and bat-eared foxes.

Habitat Wide tolerance, from desert to lush montane grassland; prefers drier areas, but occurs in locations with high rainfall.

Behaviour Nocturnal in areas where it comes into conflict with humans; in undisturbed areas moves and forages in cooler daylight hours. Mainly solitary or in mated pairs, but family parties not unusual. Pairs form long-term bond and both mark and defend the territory. Range sizes vary according to factors such as food availability and disturbance. When rearing pups, a pair is often assisted by young of previous season.

Food Wide range of food: young antelope, rodents, birds, reptiles, insects, fruit (wild and cultivated) and carrion. In sheep-farming areas some individuals take to killing lambs and sheep.

Reproduction Litter size ranges from 1–8 (usually 3–4) pups, weighing 150–200 g, born after gestation of about 60 days. Breeding is seasonal, July–October. Female has 2 pairs inguinal mammae.

Longevity Up to 14 years in captivity; rarely more than 7 years in the wild.

Calls One of the distinctive regional calls: a screaming yell, finishing off with 3 or 4 sharp yaps, often repeated. Mainly prior to and at conclusion of foraging, but male very vocal during mating season (April–August).

Occurrence Found almost throughout the region, in most conservation areas and on farmland.

MEASUREMENTS
Weight: 6–12 kg
(♂ averages heavier than ♀)
Shoulder height: 30–48 cm
Total length: 71 cm–1.3 m
Tail length: 26–40 cm

Right front

51 mm without claws

Right back

56 mm without claws

SIDE-STRIPED JACKAL

Canis adustus

Afrikaans: *Witkwasjakkals* **German:** *Streifenschakal* **French:** *Chacal à flancs rayés*

Identification pointers From a distance, more or less uniformly grey, with legs more brownish. At close quarters, light-coloured stripe or band liberally fringed with dark grey or black, along each flank. Underparts and throat usually paler. Tail quite bushy, mostly black, usually with distinct white tip. Ears smaller than those of black-backed jackal.

Similar Black-backed jackal has dark saddle and longer ears, no white tail tip.

Habitat Strong preference for well-watered and wooded areas, but not forest; avoids completely open areas.

Behaviour Mainly nocturnal, but may be active in cooler daylight hours and when overcast. Solitary animals mostly seen, but pairs and family groups are not unusual. Home range and defended territory occupied by a mating pair; ranges seem to be well spaced. In one study in the region home range sizes were 18–19 km², larger than those of black-backed jackal living in same area. More nocturnal and shyer than black-backed jackal; very little is known about their behaviour.

Food More omnivorous of the 2 jackals. Wide variety of food: small mammals, birds, reptiles, insects, carrion, and substantial quantities of wild fruit and berries. Also feed on commercial crops, such as maize, pumpkin and groundnuts.

Reproduction Litter of 3–6 pups, weighing about 200 g, born after gestation of 57–60 days. Young born August–January in the region, in burrows dug and abandoned by other species. Female has 2 pairs inguinal mammae.

Longevity 10–12 years in captivity; probably less in the wild.

Calls Most commonly heard at night is an owl-like hoot; explosive *bwaa*, cackling; pup whimpers.

Occurrence Found in far northern and eastern areas of region. Caprivi (Namibia); Chobe, Moremi, Okavango (Botswana); Hwange, Mana Pools, Gonarezhou (Zimbabwe); Kruger, iSimangaliso (South Africa); Banhine, Gorongoza (Mozambique).

MEASUREMENTS
Weight: 7.5–12 kg
Shoulder height: 40–48 cm
Total length: 96 cm–1.2 m
Tail length: 30–40 cm

Right front

43 mm without claws

Right back

47 mm without claws

AFRICAN WILD DOG

Lycaon pictus

Afrikaans: Wildehond **German:** Afrikanischer Wildhund **French:** *Lycaon*

Identification pointers Similar in size to domestic German shepherd dog, although of lighter build and longer in leg. Body is irregularly blotched with black, white, brown and a yellowish-brown; each dog has its own individual pattern. Muzzle is black, with black continuing as a line from muzzle to between ears. Ears large, rounded and dark; bushy tail usually white-tipped.
Similar Should not be misidentified, but see heavier and differently marked spotted hyaena; smaller jackals.
Habitat Open and lightly wooded savanna, moderately bushed country and, rarely, forest margins.
Behaviour Nearly all hunting takes place during day. Social, living in packs of 10–15 adults and subadults. Packs include several related adult males, and one or more related adult female/s originating from different packs. Usually only dominant pack female will successfully rear a litter of pups. Hunting is highly synchronized, with pack members working co-operatively.

Food Medium-sized mammals, chiefly antelope. In the region, springbok, impala, greater kudu, common duiker and common reedbuck of particular importance as prey.
Reproduction Litter of 7–10 pups, weighing about 365 g, born after gestation of 69–73 days. In the region, young are born during dry winter months (March–September), when grass is short and hunting conditions are at their best. All pack members guard, 'baby-sit' and regurgitate food for young at den. Female has 6–8 pairs mammae.
Longevity 10–11 years in the wild.
Calls Very vocal, with a range of calls; a far-carrying bell-like *hoo* hoot, barks, growls, bird-like twittering and whine.
Occurrence Khaudom, Caprivi (Namibia); Chobe, Okavango, Nxai Pan, Moremi (Botswana); Hwange, Mana Pools, Gonarezhou (Zimbabwe); Kruger, Mapungubwe, Madikwe, Pilanesberg, Hluhluwe-Imfolozi, iSimangaliso, Kwandwe, Greater Addo (South Africa).

MEASUREMENTS
Weight: 17–25 kg
Shoulder height: 60–75 cm
Total length: 1.05–1.5 m
Tail length: 30–40 cm

Right front

70 mm without claws

Right back

65 mm without claws

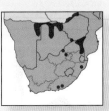

Endangered

CAPE CLAWLESS OTTER

Aonyx capensis

Afrikaans: *Groototter* **German:** *Kap-Fingerotter* **French:** *Loutre à joues blanches du Cap*

Identification pointers Larger of 2 otter species. Coat dark brown, with white fur extending from lips to upper chest; blackish appearance when wet. Legs short and stout; long tail heavy at base, tapers towards tip. Toes finger-like, partly webbed and lack claws. On land, walks with back arched. When swimming, usually only head visible.

Similar Spotted-necked otter much smaller, with white spotting on throat and upper chest. Range only overlaps in east and north. Water mongoose much smaller, with shaggy coat.

Habitat Rivers, estuaries, lakes, swamps, coastal waters and man-made dams. Frequently wanders several kilometres from water to move between suitable locations and to hunt.

Behaviour Mainly crepuscular, but activity has been recorded at all times of day and night. Usually solitary, but also pairs and small family parties. At rest lies up among dense vegetation or in self-excavated burrows (holts) in sandy soils adjacent

to water-bodies. Latrine areas, with accumulations of whitish-grey droppings, useful indication of presence. Much hunting in water relies on sight; also able to work in murky water by feeling with sensitive fingers.

Food Crabs, fish, frogs, as well as small mammals, birds, insects and molluscs.

Reproduction 1–3 (usually 1–2) cubs, weighing 200 g, born after gestation of 60–65 days. No specific season, although most births March–August in the region. Female has 2 pairs abdominal mammae.

Longevity A captive has lived to 15 years; no information on wild.

Calls Broad vocabulary; aggressive meowing wail leading to a fierce *kwa-a-a-kwaaaaa* bark; contact whistles.

Occurrence Caprivi (Namibia); Chobe, Okavango (Botswana); Gonarezhou (Zimbabwe); Kruger, Ithala, uKhahlamba, Great Fish River, Greater Addo, Garden Route, Karoo, De Hoop, Agulhas, West Coast, Cedarberg (South Africa).

MEASUREMENTS
Weight: 10–18 kg (max. 25 kg)
Shoulder height: 35 cm
Total length: 1.1–1.6 m
Tail length: 50 cm

Right front
106 mm

Right back
108 mm

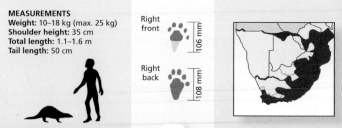

SPOTTED-NECKED OTTER

Lutra maculicollis

Afrikaans: *Kleinotter* **German:** *Fleckenhalsotter* **French:** *Loutre à cou tacheté*

Identification pointers Smaller of region's 2 otters, with a long, slender body and somewhat flattened tail. Feet fully webbed; each toe carries a distinct claw. Overall body colour is dark brown to reddish-brown; blackish appearance when wet. Throat and upper chest variably mottled and/or blotched with white or creamy-white.

Similar Cape clawless otter is much bigger, has uniform white throat. Water mongoose similar size, but with shaggy coat and long-haired tail; rarely swims.

Habitat Rivers, lakes, swamps, dams; unlike Cape clawless otter, rarely moves far from water.

Behaviour Diurnal. Associates in groups of 2–6 animals, although larger groups have been seen. Quite vocal, group members maintaining contact with whistling calls. In water they dive and 'porpoise' in much the same way as a dolphin, and can be very playful, chasing each other, and rolling over in the water. Droppings (smaller than those of Cape clawless) are deposited in regularly used latrines close to water's edge. Most prey is caught in water and usually carried to bank for eating. Relies mainly on sight for hunting; clear water is essential – will soon disappear from heavily silted waters. A number of South Africa's rivers once inhabited by this otter are now too silt-laden and polluted to sustain them.

Food Mostly fish, but also takes crabs, insects, frogs and birds.

Reproduction 2–3 cubs born after gestation of about 60 days. Births possibly year-round, but no information from region. Female has 2 pairs abdominal mammae.

Longevity Not known.

Calls Whistles, mewing *yea-ea-ea-ea*, squeaks and bird-like twittering.

Occurrence Fairly limited range in southern Africa; has disappeared from several silted or polluted rivers in South Africa. Caprivi (Namibia); Chobe, Moremi, Okavango (Botswana); Kruger, uKhahlamba (South Africa).

MEASUREMENTS
Weight: 3–5 kg
Shoulder height: < 30 cm
Total length: < 1 m
Tail length: 30–50 cm

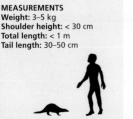

Right front

Right back

58 mm without claws

70 mm without claws

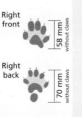

HONEY BADGER (RATEL)

Mellivora capensis

Afrikaans: *Ratel* **German:** *Honigdachs* **French:** *Ratel*

Identification pointers Thickset, stocky and relatively short-legged, with short, bushy tail that is usually held erect when on the move. Upperparts are silvery-grey; underparts, legs and front of face are black. Band of white usually separates upperparts from underparts, converging on top of head and on down to tail. Feet are large and powerful, with long claws on front feet. Eyes are quite small and ears tiny.

Similar See much smaller striped polecat.

Habitat Virtually all habitats, but favours rocky hill country, open savanna types, as well as flood plains. Occupies most of coastal plain except in Namibia.

Behaviour Mostly nocturnal, but may be seen in cooler daylight hours in undisturbed areas. Usually seen singly, but pairs and female with young may be observed. Tough and potentially aggressive; has been recorded attacking species as large as elephant, buffalo and humans, but only when threatened.

Food Mainly invertebrates (insects, spiders, scorpions), but rodents, reptiles, birds, carrion and some wild fruit eaten. Name comes from tendency to break into beehives and eat honey and bee larvae.

Reproduction Litter of 1–2 pups born after gestation of about 62–74 days, although not confirmed. From limited information, young appear to be born any time of year. Often only 1 pup is reared successfully. Female has 2 pairs inguinal mammae.

Longevity 26 years in captivity.

Calls Seldom heard, but a range of growls, screams, grunts, barks and whines.

Occurrence Etosha, Khaudom, Caprivi (Namibia); Chobe, Okavango, Nxai Pan, Makgadikgadi, Central Kalahari (Botswana); Gonarezhou, Hwange, Mana Pools (Zimbabwe); Banhine, Gorongoza (Mozambique); Kruger, Mapungubwe, Madikwe, Marokele, Pilanesberg, Kgalagadi, Augrabies, Namaqua, West Coast, Agulhas, Garden Route, Greater Addo, Ithala, uMkhuze (South Africa).

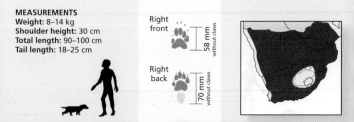

MEASUREMENTS
Weight: 8–14 kg
Shoulder height: 30 cm
Total length: 90–100 cm
Tail length: 18–25 cm

Right front
58 mm without claws

Right back
70 mm without claws

STRIPED POLECAT

Ictonyx striatus

Afrikaans: *Stinkmuishond* **German:** *Zorilla* **French:** *Zorille commun*

Identification pointers Conspicuous black-and-white markings, which serve as warning to would-be predators. Relatively long body hair is shiny black, with 4 distinct white stripes from top of head to base of tail along back and flanks. White patch on forehead between eyes, and a larger white patch at base of ear. Tail predominantly white, but black shows through.

Similar Only striped weasel (*Poecilogale albinucha*), mainly in east, could be confused with it; smaller, with very short legs and body hair, top of head all white.

Habitat Very wide tolerance; absent only from true forest and coastal Namib Desert.

Behaviour Strictly nocturnal, emerging after dark. Usually solitary, but pairs and female accompanied by young sometimes seen. During the day they shelter in burrows dug by other species, among rocks, dense vegetation and even in association with man-made structures. When no other shelter available, capable of digging own burrows. Main defence is to spray attacker with foul-smelling fluid from anal glands; under extreme threat will sham death.

Food Mainly insects and rodents, but also other small animals.

Reproduction Litter of 1–5 (usually 1–3) pups, weighing 10–15 g, born after 36-day gestation. Birth season not known for the region; most probably in summer, but some records include winter births. Copulation may last for well over an hour. Female has 1 pair inguinal, 1 pair abdominal mammae.

Longevity 5.5 years in captivity.

Calls Has considerable repertoire: growls, bark-scream, high scream; young purr-chirrup; seldom heard unless cornered or threatened.

Occurrence Present in virtually all conservation areas and elsewhere. Very widespread in the region and able to adapt to human habitat modification. Frequently seen dead on roads.

MEASUREMENTS
Weight: 600 g–1.4 kg
(♂ larger than ♀)
Shoulder height: 10–15 cm
Total length: 57–67 cm
Tail length: 26 cm

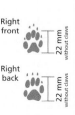

Right front

Right back

22 mm without claws

22 mm without claws

BANDED MONGOOSE

Mungos mungo

Afrikaans: *Gebande muishond* **German:** *Zebramanguste* **French:** *Mangouste rayée*

Identification pointers Rather small, with distinctive markings. Body colour varies from grizzled-grey to grey-brown, with 10–12 dark brown to black transverse bands on back running from just behind shoulders to base of tail. Fairly bushy tail, usually somewhat darker towards the tip. Head quite long and pointed, with short, rounded ears. Two subspecies dubiously recognized, with lighter coloured animals in northwest, darker in southeast.

Similar Very little range overlap but see suricate.

Habitat Wide tolerance, but avoids extremely dry areas (usually > 500 mm rainfall).

Behaviour Strictly diurnal, spending nights in holes, especially in termite mounds, of which several are utilized within home range. Social, living in troops of 5–30 individuals, sometimes more. Range size varies according to number of troop members and food abundance, but ranges from 80 ha to > 400 ha.

Encounters between troops may result in conflict, but they do not defend territories. Frequently mark rocks, logs and other troop members with secretions from anal glands.

Food Mainly insects and other invertebrates, also small vertebrates.

Reproduction 2–6 young, weighing 20 g average, born after gestation of about 60 days. Breeding usually synchronized within a troop. Most litters born during summer rains (October–February). Young may suckle from any lactating female. Female has 3 pairs abdominal mammae.

Longevity 11 years in captivity; < 10 years in the wild.

Calls Most commonly heard is grunt-chitter *churr* when the troop is foraging.

Occurrence Etosha, Khaudom, Caprivi (Namibia); Chobe, Okavango, Moremi (Botswana); Gonarezhou, Hwange, Mana Pools (Zimbabwe); Banhine, Gorongoza (Mozambique); Kruger, Mapungubwe, Madikwe, Marakele, Ndumo, uMkhuze, Hluhluwe-Imfolozi, Kgalagadi (South Africa).

MEASUREMENTS
Weight: 1–1.6 kg
Shoulder height: 18–20 cm
Total length: 50–65 cm
Tail length: 18–20 cm

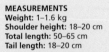

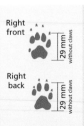

Right front — 29 mm without claws

Right back — 29 mm without claws

SMALL (CAPE) GREY MONGOOSE

Galerella pulverulenta

Afrikaans: *Kleingrysmuishond* **German:** *Kleinichneumon, Kapmanguste* **French:** *Mangouste grise du Cap*

Identification pointers Small, with uniform grizzled-grey colouring that may be brown-grey in northwest, paler grey in south and darker grey in east. These forms designated as subspecies, but may not be valid as there is much variation. Legs darker than rest of body; bushy tail similar in colour to body. Head quite long, muzzle pointed. When moving, holds tail parallel to ground.

Similar Large grey mongoose much bigger, with black-tipped tail. Marginally overlaps range of slender mongoose in north, but this species less stocky, in the region more rufous, and has black-tipped tail held curled towards back when running.

Habitat Wide habitat tolerance, from forest to open scrub. Particularly common in southern coastal areas and adjacent interior.

Behaviour Active by day, although tends to lie up during hottest part of day in summer. Daytime and night-time retreats include old burrows, dense vegetation, stone walls and rock piles. Usually solitary, but pairs and family parties (female and young) occasionally seen. Regularly uses same pathways within home ranges of between 5 ha and > 90 ha. Home ranges overlap considerably. Although this mongoose marks range with glandular secretions, it is not known whether it is territorial.

Food Invertebrates (mainly insects) and small rodents; also carrion, birds, reptiles, amphibians and small quantities of wild fruit.

Reproduction 1–3 young born about August–December in south of range, in holes among rocks or in dense vegetation. Female has 3 pairs abdominal mammae.

Longevity A captive lived 8 years 8 months.

Calls Adult gives hiss-bark and snarls when caught in cage traps; half-grown young gives low purr-call.

Occurrence Richtersveld, Namaqua, Augrabies, Cedarberg, West Coast, Table Mountain, Agulhas, Karoo, Garden Route, Greater Addo, Camdeboo, Mountain Zebra, Great Fish River, Golden Gate (South Africa).

MEASUREMENTS
Weight: 500 g–1 kg
Shoulder height: 10–12 cm
Total length: 55–69 cm
Tail length: 20–34 cm

Right front

25 mm without claws

Right back

28 mm without claws

SLENDER MONGOOSE

Galerella sanguinea

Afrikaans: *Swartkwasmuishond* **German:** *Schlankichneumon, Schlankmanguste*
French: *Mangouste rouge, Mangouste svelte*

Identification pointers Small, very slender and long-tailed. Three subspecies sometimes recognized in the region, but all have a black-tipped tail, held slightly curved upwards at tip, or over back when running. Over much of range dominant colour is greyish-brown to grey-yellow, but in south most animals are reddish-orange to buffy-brown, often heavily 'pencilled' with black; in northern Namibia dark red-brown is dominant.

Similar Dwarf mongoose has shorter tail, without black tip, and lives in troops. Small grey mongoose uniform grizzled grey; minimal overlap in south. Yellow mongoose usually has white-tipped tail.

Habitat Areas of low and high rainfall, but usually absent from forest. Penetrates arid areas along watercourses and where there are stands of scrub and thicket.

Behaviour Apparently strictly diurnal, lying up at night among dense vegetation, rock piles or in holes dug by other animals (springhares, ground squirrels). Usually solitary, but pairs run together for short periods during mating season. Probably territorial, with a male's territory overlapping those of several females. Mainly terrestrial, but a capable climber: ascends into bushes and low trees with great agility. Stalk-and-pounce hunter, approaching very close to prey and lunging at it.

Food Possible regional differences, but takes large quantities of rats and mice, insects, other invertebrates, reptiles and birds. Very occasionally eats wild fruit and berries.

Reproduction Litter of 1–2 (rarely 3) pups born after gestation of about 45 days. Probably seasonal breeders, linked to summer rains (October–February). Female has 2–3 pairs abdominal mammae.

Longevity 4–6 years estimated.

Calls Seldom heard; harsh *tschaarrr* alarm growl in cage trap, whine.

Occurrence Common in all conservation areas and on farmland through its range.

MEASUREMENTS
Weight: 370–800 g
Shoulder height: 10 cm
Total length: 50–65 cm
Tail length: 23–30 cm

Right front

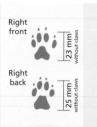

23 mm without claws

Right back

25 mm without claws

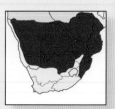

WHITE-TAILED MONGOOSE

Ichneumia albicauda

Afrikaans: *Witstertmuishond* **German:** *Weißschwanzmanguste* **French:** *Mangouste à queue blanche*

Identification pointers One of the largest mongooses in the region; walks with rump higher than shoulders and head usually held low. Legs are long, and back is slightly arched when on the move. Coarse, shaggy coat is brown-grey with grizzled appearance, but legs are black. Bushy white tail is distinctive; black-tailed specimen may occasionally be seen.

Similar Selous's mongoose much smaller and tail less distinctly white.

Habitat Preference for woodland savanna and forest margins, especially in well-watered areas; penetrates drier areas along watercourses.

Behaviour Nocturnal; lies up during day in burrows dug by other species, or in rock crevices, holes in termite mounds, or among dense vegetation. Largely solitary, although pairs and female with young may be seen. Home range size outside region has been recorded as 23–39 ha (no study in southern Africa). Both sexes territorial, although 2–3 females and their young may live in loosely knit clans.

Food Insects and other invertebrates make up most important part of diet. Also hunts rodents, birds and reptiles; largest prey includes hares and cane-rats.

Reproduction Litter of 1–2 (rarely 3–4) young born in burrow, ventilation shaft of termitaria, or in large fallen log. Birth season not well-known; most births probably coincide with summer rains, when food is most abundant. Female has 3 pairs abdominal mammae.

Longevity A captive lived 12.5 years; probably less in the wild.

Calls Muttering while foraging, purrs, whimpers, growls, scream-shrieks and harsh barks (usually when threatened).

Occurrence Caprivi (Namibia); Chobe, Okavango (Botswana); Hwange, Matobo, Mana Pools, Gonarezhou (Zimbabwe); Banhine, Maputo Elephant, Gorongoza (Mozambique); Kruger, Madikwe, Golden Gate, iSimangaliso, Ndumo, uMkhuze, uKhahlamba (South Africa).

MEASUREMENTS
Weight: 3.5–5.2 kg
Shoulder height: 25 cm
Total length: 90 cm–1.5 m
Tail length: 35–48 cm

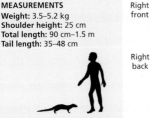

Right front

Right back

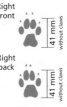

41 mm without claws

41 mm without claws

LARGE GREY MONGOOSE

Herpestes ichneumon

Afrikaans: *Grootgrysmuishond* **German:** *Ichneumon* **French:** *Mangouste ichneumon*

Identification pointers Large, with long, grey-grizzled body hair. Tail is long, bushy towards base and prominently black-tipped; when on the move tail tip is curved upwards away from ground. Lower part of legs short-haired and black. Head relatively long, but typically mongoose-like.

Similar Small grey mongoose much smaller, lacks black-tipped tail.

Habitat Vegetation around rivers, lakes, dams and marshes; also along oceanic coastlines. May wander several kilometres from usual habitat when foraging.

Behaviour Mainly diurnal, although nocturnal activity has been recorded. Usually solitary or in pairs, but family parties not uncommon. Such parties may walk in a line, nose to anus, in a snaking fashion. Frequently stands on its hind legs to view surrounding area. Droppings deposited at regularly used latrine sites; also marks rocks, logs and the like within its home range with anal gland secretions.

Food Small rodents very important in diet, but also eats other small mammals, reptiles, birds, amphibians and a wide range of invertebrates, as well as some wild fruit. Known to eat snakes.

Reproduction Litter size reported as 2–4, born after gestation of about 75 days (some records suggest as little as 60 days). Young are probably born in summer months in the region. Female usually has 2 pairs (rarely 3) abdominal mammae.

Longevity A captive lived nearly 13 years.

Calls When alarmed, or caught in cage trap, growls and snarls; normally silent.

Occurrence In the region mainly restricted to the coastal belt, extending inland to northern Zimbabwe and Botswana. Seems to be spreading range. Caprivi (Namibia); Okavango, Chobe (Botswana); Mana Pools (Zimbabwe); Kruger, Ndumo, Thembe, iSimangaliso, uKhahlamba, Greater Addo, Garden Route, Agulhas, De Hoop (South Africa).

MEASUREMENTS
Weight: 2.5–4 kg
Shoulder height: 20 cm
Total length: 1–1.1 m
Tail length: 45–58 cm

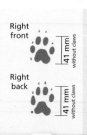

Right front
41 mm without claws

Right back
41 mm without claws

WATER MONGOOSE

Atilax paludinosus

Afrikaans: *Kommetjiegatmuishond* **German:** *Sumpfmanguste* **French:** *Mangouste des marais*

Identification pointers Large, stoutly built, with shaggy, uniformly dark brown coat. Some individuals may be almost black or reddish-brown, but all look blackish from a distance; at close quarters looks grizzled, coat often has a sheen. Hair on muzzle and feet is short, but long and erectile on tail.

Similar Spotted-necked otter similar size, with short, sleek coat and white-spotted throat. Cape clawless otter much larger, with short-haired coat.

Habitat Most well-watered habitats, rivers, marshes, swamps, lake fringes and coastline. Will penetrate arid areas along watercourses if permanent pools present.

Behaviour Nocturnal, crepuscular and terrestrial. Mostly solitary, although pairs and females with young sometimes seen. Probably territorial. When foraging follows well-used pathways. Droppings deposited at latrine sites, usually near water. Relies on sight and hearing when hunting. Long toes on front feet are very sensitive, used to probe under and among rocks for prey. Will also dig prey out of mud, especially freshwater crabs.

Food Mainly crabs and amphibians, but also a wide range of invertebrates, small rodents, birds; occasionally wild fruit.

Reproduction 1–3 young, weighing about 120 g, born in burrows, rock crevices, or among dense vegetation, after gestation of about 74 days. Births recorded from August to December. Female has 2 or 3 pairs abdominal mammae.

Longevity A captive lived 17 years 5 months; no records from wild.

Calls Growls; young gives soft, cat-like meow; explosive hiss when threatened.

Occurrence Caprivi (Namibia); Chobe, Okavango (Botswana); Gonarezhou, Mana Pools (Zimbabwe); Kruger, Mapungubwe, Ndumo, iSimangaliso, Ithala, uMkhuze, Hluhluwe-iMfolozi, uKhahlamba, Golden Gate, Willem Pretorius, Greater Addo, Great Fish River, Camdeboo, Garden Route, Agulhas, Karoo, Augrabies (South Africa).

MEASUREMENTS
Weight: 2.5–5.5 kg
Shoulder height: 22 cm
Total length: 80 cm–1 m
Tail length: 30–40 cm

Right front

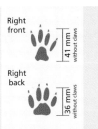

41 mm without claws

Right back

36 mm without claws

DWARF MONGOOSE

Helogale parvula

Afrikaans: *Dwergmuishond* **German:** *Südlicher Zwergichneumon* **French:** *Mangouste naine du Sud*

Identification pointers Region's smallest mongoose. Fairly short but sleek, glossy coat, ranging from dark brown to grey-brown; from close-up has slightly grizzled appearance. Three subspecies sometimes recognized in the region based on colour differences. Upper feet, throat and muzzle often more fawn to reddish. Tail same colour as body, well-haired but not bushy.

Similar Slender mongoose has longer tail, with black tip held erect or curved over body when running; this species solitary, dwarf mongoose group-living.

Habitat Open woodland and sparsely wooded savanna, as well as rocky areas within these habitats, such as on Soutpansberg.

Behaviour Strictly diurnal and terrestrial. Highly social, living in troops of 10–40 individuals. Troop occupies fixed home range of 2–30 ha. Within each troop has up to 20 den sites, often within termite mounds or among rocks. Every troop has a dominant male and female and, unusually,

females are dominant over males. Only dominant female breeds, but all troop members care for young. Often basks after emerging from den. As with banded mongoose and suricate, troop members maintain contact with a constant 'chatter'.

Food Mainly insects, other invertebrates and, to a lesser extent, small reptiles, birds and their eggs.

Reproduction Litter of 1–7 (average 2–4) young born after gestation of 50–54 days. Births occur mainly in rainy season (October–March). Female has 3 pairs abdominal mammae.

Longevity Up to 10 years in captivity; 7 years in the wild.

Calls Most commonly heard are *peep* and twitter contact calls; *tchee* and *tchrr* alarm calls.

Occurrence Etosha, Caprivi (Namibia); Okavango, Chobe (Botswana); Hwange, Mana Pools (Zimbabwe); Mapungubwe, Madikwe, Marakele, Kruger, Ndumo, Thembe (South Africa).

MEASUREMENTS
Weight: 220–350 g
Shoulder height: 7 cm
Total length: 35–40 cm
Tail length: 14–20 cm

Right front

16 mm without claws

Right back

16 mm without claws

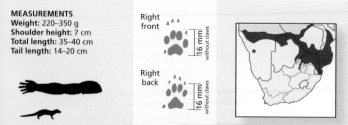

YELLOW MONGOOSE

Cynictis penicillata

Afrikaans: *Rooimeerkat* **German:** *Fuchsmanguste* **French:** *Mangouste fauve*

Identification pointers Fairly small. Usually reddish-yellow to tawny-yellow in overall colour, often grizzled appearance, with prominent white tip to tail in south of range; more northerly animals more greyish in colour and often lack white tail-tip. Several subspecies sometimes recognized, but there is much variation, each tending to blend into the other making identification or separation difficult. Tail quite bushy, held parallel to ground when walking, and at 45° to ground when running. Chin, throat and upper chest paler to off-white. Eyes are orange-brown.

Similar In extreme north of range, Selous's mongoose. Slender mongoose has black-tipped tail, held curved when running; mainly solitary.

Habitat Open grassland and semi-desert scrub, agricultural land; also, in some areas, open woodland with grass cover.

Behaviour Diurnal. Normally forages alone, but lives communally in warrens of 5–10 individuals (rarely as many as 20). Will dig own burrows, but readily occupies those dug by suricate and ground squirrels, sometimes with all 3 species sharing same burrow systems. Each morning individuals disperse to forage along regularly used pathways. Deposits droppings in latrines in close proximity to burrow entrances.

Food Mostly insects and other invertebrates, but also takes small rodents, amphibians, reptiles and birds.

Reproduction Litter of 2–5 young born after gestation of 60–62 days. Young born October–January in southern part of range, extending through to March in north. Female has 3 pairs abdominal mammae.

Longevity 12 years in captivity; probably considerably less in the wild.

Calls Purr, scream and low growl.

Occurrence Easy to see in Etosha, Khaudom (Namibia); Central Kalahari, Chobe, Nxai Pan (Botswana); Kgalagadi, Augrabies, Namaqua, Karoo, Greater Addo (South Africa).

MEASUREMENTS
Weight: 450–900 g
Shoulder height: 15–18 cm
Total length: 40–60 cm
Tail length: 18–25 cm

Right front
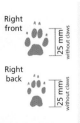
25 mm without claws

Right back
25 mm without claws

SURICATE (MEERKAT)

Suricata suricatta

Afrikaans: *Stokstertmeerkat* **German:** *Surikate, Erdmännchen* **French:** *Suricate*

Identification pointers Relatively small, with long, wedge-shaped muzzle. Body fawn to silvery-grey (lighter coloured in northwest) with a number of darker, irregular transverse bars running from behind shoulders to base of tail. Two subspecies (based on minor colour variations) sometimes recognized. Tail is thin, tapering and short-haired, with dark tip; held vertically when running. Long front claws. Small, rounded ears.

Similar Banded mongoose has complete back-bars; minimal range overlap.

Habitat Open, dry and lightly vegetated country; avoids dense bush.

Behaviour Diurnal, emerging from burrows only after sunrise, returning before sunset. Usually lives in groups of 8–15 individuals, but groups can number from 5 to 40. Will dig its own burrow complexes (warrens), but also utilizes those dug by ground squirrels and yellow mongooses; often lives in harmony with these species. When foraging or on the move, group maintains contact with constant, soft grunting call. Commonly stands on hind legs, using tail as a 'prop', when basking or on alert for predators or rival troops.

Food Mainly insects, other invertebrates, reptiles and birds.

Reproduction 2–5 pups, weighing 25–36 g, born after gestation of about 73 days. Mainly born in summer (October–March), but records exist for other times. All troop members care for young. In many troops dominant female produces most litters. Female has 3 pairs abdominal mammae.

Longevity Up to 12 years in captivity; probably considerably less in the wild.

Calls Grunts and 'mumbles' among troop members while foraging, or at rest; alarm bark; hiss.

Occurrence In virtually every conservation area in range and common on farmland. Some good observation locations include Kgalagadi Transfrontier Park, Karoo, Greater Addo (South Africa).

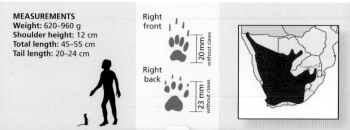

MEASUREMENTS
Weight: 620–960 g
Shoulder height: 12 cm
Total length: 45–55 cm
Tail length: 20–24 cm

Right front
20 mm without claws

Right back
23 mm without claws

1 COMMON LARGE-SPOTTED GENET *Genetta maculata*
2 SOUTH AFRICAN LARGE-SPOTTED GENET *Genetta tigrina*

Afrikaans: *Rooikolmuskeljaatkat, Grootkolmuskeljaatkat* **German:** *Pantherginsterkatze, Großfleckginsterkatze* **French:** *Genette pardine*

Identification pointers Previously considered to be subspecies, but now each has full species status due to recent findings. Long, slender body and well-haired, long tail with rings and black tip. Common large-spotted has rusty-brown spots and blotches; South African large-spotted has much darker to black spots and blotches. Chin and lips usually white; white patch below each eye. Ears long and rounded. Claws retractile like those of cat.

Similar Small-spotted genet found in arid areas; has overall greyish-grizzled coat with numerous small black spots and bars; erectile crest along back, absent in large-spotted genets. Only small-spotted genet found in arid habitats.

Habitat Well-watered areas with dense vegetation, such as forest, woodland, coastal thicket, riparian woodland and fynbos; rarely in areas with < 500 mm annual rainfall.

Behaviour Nocturnal, lying up under cover during day. Most hunting done on ground, but excellent climber. Normally solitary, but pairs and female with young occasionally seen. Droppings deposited at latrine sites, usually in open or conspicuous places.

Food Invertebrates, especially insects, but also small rodents, reptiles, amphibians and birds. Largest prey records include young hares and cane-rats.

Reproduction 2–4 pups (rarely to 5), weighing 50–80 g, born after gestation of about 70 days. Births mainly in spring/summer months (September–March). Female has 2 pairs abdominal mammae.

Longevity 14 years in captivity; less in the wild.

Calls Seldom heard, but various combinations of growling, coughs, spitting, purring and meowing.

Occurrence Common, widespread, in most conservation areas with suitable habitat.

MEASUREMENTS
Weight: 1.8–3.2 kg
Shoulder height: 18–22 cm
Total length: 85 cm–1.1 m
Tail length: 40–50 cm

Right front
22 mm

Right back
20 mm

■ *Genetta maculata*
■ *Genetta tigrina*

SMALL-SPOTTED GENET

Genetta genetta

Afrikaans: *Kleinkolmuskejaatkat* **German:** *Kleinfleckginsterkatze* **French:** *Genette commune*

Identification pointers Long, slender body and short legs. Tail is long, ringed with black and greyish-white, usually with a white tip. Overall colour off-white to greyish-white, with numerous small black spots and bars. Long, rounded ears and rather pointed face with black-and-white markings (white patch under eye). Crest of fairly long erectile hair runs from nape to base of tail.

Similar Large-spotted genet has different coat colour, larger black or rusty-brown spots; no erectile crest. African civet much larger, longer legged, shorter tailed.

Habitat Very wide habitat tolerance, ranging from margins of arid areas to those of high rainfall, but seldom in true forest. Mainly woodland, riverine margins, as well as isolated rock outcrops on open plains.

Behaviour Exclusively nocturnal; spends day lying up among dense vegetation, and in rock crevices and burrows dug by other mammals. Solitary; only rarely are pairs or females with young seen. Perhaps more terrestrial than large-spotted genets, but still an agile and able climber. Droppings deposited at latrine sites, usually on exposed location, such as raised rock ledge or log, indicating that they serve to mark home range and, possibly, territory.

Food Invertebrates, particularly insects, and will take small mammals, birds, reptiles, frogs and some wild fruit.

Reproduction 2–4 young, weighing 50–80 g, born after gestation of about 70 days. Birthing mainly in summer. Female has 2 pairs abdominal mammae.

Longevity > 9 years in captivity.

Calls Very similar to large-spotted genet's; cat-like call sequences.

Occurrence Occurs in most reserves and widely on farmland within its range in the region. Common and widespread, even in areas of quite high human density. Will den in attics of houses and in cluttered outbuildings.

MEASUREMENTS
Weight: 1.5–2.6 kg
Shoulder height: 18–20 cm
Total length: 86 cm–1 m
Tail length: 40–50 cm

Right front

Right back

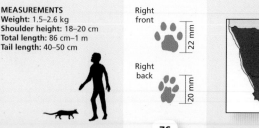

AFRICAN CIVET

Civettictis civetta

Afrikaans: *Sivet* **German:** *Afrikanische Zibetkatze* **French:** *Civette africaine*

Identification pointers About the size of a medium dog (spaniel). Long-bodied, long-legged, heavily built. When walking, head held low, tail usually horizontal or slightly drooping. Hair long and coarse. Overall greyish to grey-brown, with many black spots, blotches and bands. Light grey forehead, white muzzle and dark-ringed eyes. Distinct light band from ear base towards chest. Legs black. Tail banded white and black below; black upperside and tip. Ridge of dark erectile hair runs along spine to tail.

Similar Genets are smaller, with longer tail and shorter legs.

Habitat Wide tolerance, with preference for more densely wooded and forested areas; nearly always close to water.

Behaviour Mainly nocturnal, but seen in cooler daylight hours and on overcast days in undisturbed areas. Solitary forager, but occasionally pairs seen, or female with well-grown pups. Regularly used dung middens/latrines ('civetries') around range; often located along paths and roadways. Also marks range with dark anal gland secretions, pasted on grass stalks, twigs and even rocks.

Food Mainly invertebrates, chiefly insects, also small rodents, hares, birds, reptiles, carrion and large quantities of wild fruit; wild dates in some areas.

Reproduction 2–4 pups, weighing about 325 g, born after gestation of 60–65 days. Birthing during summer months (August–January). Female has 2 pairs abdominal mammae.

Longevity A captive lived 15 years; probably < 10 years in the wild.

Calls Contact *ha-ha-ha*, cat-like meow, growls, cough-spit and scream. Seldom heard calling in the wild.

Occurrence Always at low densities. Skeleton Coast, Caprivi (Namibia); Chobe, Okavango (Botswana); Hwange, Matobo, Mana Pools, Gonarezhou (Zimbabwe); Mapungubwe, Marakele, Kruger, Ndumo, iSimangaliso (South Africa); Banhine, Gorongoza (Mozambique).

MEASUREMENTS
Weight: 9–15 kg
Shoulder height: 40 cm
Total length: 1.2–1.4 m
Tail length: 40–50 cm

Right front

Right back

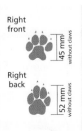

45 mm without claws

52 mm without claws

77

SPOTTED HYAENA

Crocuta crocuta

Afrikaans: *Gevlekte hiëna* **German:** *Tüpfelhyäne* **French:** *Hyène tachetée*

Identification pointers Most commonly seen hyaena in the region. Heavily built forequarters stand higher than rump. Large head, with prominent rounded ears and black muzzle. Colour ranges from fawn-yellow to grey-fawn, with scattering of dark brown spots and blotches. Head, throat and chest not spotted. Tail short, held erect or curved over back at times.

Similar Brown hyaena has more shaggy coat, no spots and long, pointed ears; not in packs. Aardwolf much smaller, striped and lacks spots.

Habitat Open and lightly wooded savanna, denser woodland types and rugged, broken country.

Behaviour Nocturnal and diurnal. Usually lives in family groups, or clans, led by an adult female. Clan size ranges from 3 to > 15 individuals living within defended territory. Each clan regularly marks its territory with communal dung middens, secretions from anal glands. Skilled hunters, and will drive other predators from kills.

Food Mainly antelope, but also plains zebra and buffalo; carrion.

Reproduction 1–2 cubs (occasionally 3), weighing about 1.5 kg, born after gestation of about 110 days. Cubs born in burrow or road culvert any time of year, but with peak during summer rains. Female has 2 pairs abdominal mammae.

Longevity 12–25 years in captivity; > 16 years in the wild.

Calls Most characteristic set of calls heard in savanna areas; *who-oop*, giggles, yells, growls, grunt-laughs, whines and soft squeals.

Occurrence Namib-Naukluft, Skeleton Coast, Etosha, Khaudom, Caprivi (Namibia); Chobe, Okavango, Moremi, Central Kalahari, Nxai Pan, Makgadikgadi (Botswana); Hwange, Mana Pools, Gonarezhou (Zimbabwe); Banhine, Gorongoza (Mozambique); Mapungubwe, Marakele, Madikwe, Pilanesberg, Kruger, uMkhuze, iSimangaliso, Hluhluwe-Imfolozi, Kgalagadi, Greater Addo (South Africa).

MEASUREMENTS
Weight: 60–80 kg
Shoulder height: 85 cm
Total length: 1.2–1.8 m
Tail length: 25 cm

Right front
96 mm without claws

Right back
89 mm without claws

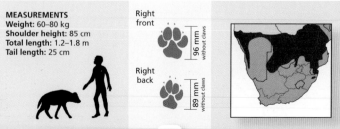

BROWN HYAENA

Parahyaena brunnea

Afrikaans: *Strandjut* **German:** *Schabrackenhyäne, Braune Hyäne* **French:** *Hyène brune*

Identification pointers Large size, with shoulders higher than rump. Large head with long, pointed ears. Body covered with long, shaggy coat, with a dense mantle of hair on back and shoulders. Mantle lighter in colour than rest of body. Overall body colour varies from light brown to dark brown; legs ringed alternately black and light brown. Tail short, bushy and dark.

Similar Spotted hyaena has short coat, no mantle, spotted and blotched, rounded ears. Aardwolf much smaller, lighter coat colour, transverse body stripes.

Habitat Mainly in drier parts of region, including Namib Desert and Kalahari, but previously occupied virtually all habitats. In mountainous areas within woodland savanna and southern coastal plain.

Behaviour Nocturnal and crepuscular, but sometimes seen during daylight hours. Solitary animals usually seen, but several animals may share a territory. Territory size varies considerably, from about 19 km² in one study to between 235 km² and 480 km² in Kalahari. Territory is shared by an extended family unit of 4–6 animals, all assist in raising cubs.

Food Mainly scavenges, also eats a wide variety of small vertebrates (including young antelope), insects and wild fruit.

Reproduction 1–5 pups (usually 2–3), weighing about 750 g, born after gestation of about 90 days. Female has 2 pairs abdominal mammae.

Longevity A captive lived > 29 years; at least 12 years in the wild.

Calls Less vocal than spotted hyaena; range of growls, snarls, whimpers, yelps and squeals.

Occurrence Skeleton Coast, Namib-Naukluft, Etosha, Khaudom (Namibia); Chobe, Central Kalahari, Makgadikgadi, Nxai Pan (Botswana); Hwange (Zimbabwe); Kgalagadi, Augrabies, Pilanesberg, Madikwe, Mapungubwe, Marakele, Kruger, iSimangaliso, Hluhluwe-Imfolozi, Greater Addo (South Africa).

MEASUREMENTS
Weight: ♂ 35–58 kg (average 47 kg); ♀ 28–47 kg (average 42 kg)
Shoulder height: 80 cm
Total length: 1.3–1.6 m
Tail length: 17–30 cm

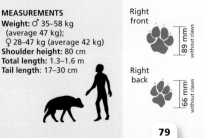

Right front

89 mm without claws

Right back

66 mm without claws

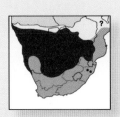

AARDWOLF

Proteles cristatus

Afrikaans: *Maanhaarjakkals, Erdwolf* **German:** *Erdwolf* **French:** *Protèle*

Identification pointers Medium-sized, higher at shoulders than rump, but not as pronounced as in hyaenas. Coat coarse and longish; mane of erectile hair on neck and back, raised when animal is under stress. Colour ranges from pale tawny to yellow-white, several vertical black stripes on body, black bands on upper part of legs. Muzzle, feet and much of tail black. Ears large and pointed.

Similar Spotted hyaena much larger, shorter hair, lacks stripes, rounded ears. Brown hyaena larger, lacks body stripes, shaggier coat.

Habitat Wide tolerance, from low to high rainfall, with range dependent on availability of its principal food, termites.

Behaviour Mainly nocturnal and crepuscular, but active on overcast days in undisturbed areas. Normally a solitary forager, but pairs and family parties occasionally seen. Two or more animals occupy a home range, with droppings deposited in shallow scrapes at latrine sites. Territories are usually maintained and defended by a mated pair. Several females may drop their pups in the same den, usually in burrows excavated by other species.

Food Termites, especially harvesters and particularly *Trinervitermes* species, make up bulk of diet. One calculation suggests a single aardwolf may consume 105 million termites (some 420 kg) in a year.

Reproduction 1–4 pups, weighing about 50 g, born after gestation of some 90 days. Most litters in South Africa born October–December; more extended further north. Female has 2 pairs inguinal mammae.

Longevity A captive lived 15 years.

Calls Seldom heard, but if cornered or injured gives an impressive roar, out of proportion to its size; barks, growls, snarls, whimpers.

Occurrence Occurs across much of the region but absent from the Namib Desert and Mozambique coastal plain. In most conservation areas in the region.

MEASUREMENTS
Weight: 6–11 kg
Shoulder height: 50 cm
Total length: 84 cm–1 m
Tail length: 20–28 cm

Right front
60 mm without claws

Right back
53 mm without claws

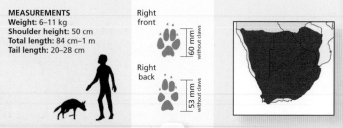

AFRICAN WILD CAT

Felis silvestris lybica

Afrikaans: *Vaalboskat* **German:** *Afrikanische Wildkatze* **French:** *Chat sauvage d'Afrique*

Identification pointers Similar in appearance to domestic cat, but larger with longer legs. Colour pale sandy-brown in drier areas to light or dark grey in wetter parts. Body marked with more or less distinct dark, vertical stripes. Relatively long tail, dark-ringed with black tip. Chin and throat white; chest and inner thighs usually lighter colour. Back of ears rich to dull reddish-brown.

Similar Domestic or feral cats and hybrids lack reddish backs to ears. Small spotted cat smaller, shorter tail, distinctive dark spots.

Habitat Desert to high-rainfall montane areas, woodland, forest fringes, grassland and broken, rocky country.

Behaviour Mainly nocturnal and crepuscular, but occasionally seen on cool, overcast days. During the day lies up in rock crevices, among dense vegetation, in burrows excavated by other species and in trees. Solitary, except when pair comes together for mating, or female accompanied by young. Both sexes establish, mark and defend territories. Droppings usually buried, but small surface middens are used in some areas. They are stalk-wait-pounce hunters.

Food Small rodents make up bulk of diet, but also mammals up to the size of hares, springhares and young rock hyrax. Occasionally takes young of small antelope, ostrich chicks, bustards, smaller birds, as well as reptiles and insects.

Reproduction 1–5 kittens, weighing 40–50 g, born after gestation of 56–65 days. Most births recorded during warm, wet summer months across much of region, some recorded in other months. Female has 3–4 pairs abdominal mammae.

Longevity Up to 15 years in captivity; no information on wild.

Calls Very similar repertoire to domestic cat; snarls, hiss, spit, yowl, purr.

Occurrence Absent only from Namib Desert coastal strip, but purity of populations has been compromised by inter-breeding with domestic cats. Found in virtually all conservation areas within its range.

MEASUREMENTS
Weight: 2.5–6 kg
Shoulder height: 35 cm
Total length: 85 cm–1 m
Tail length: 25–37 cm

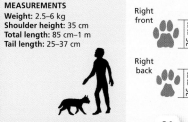

Right front

Right back

36 mm

36 mm

SMALL SPOTTED CAT

Felis nigripes

Afrikaans: *Swartpootkat* **German:** *Schwarzfußkatze* **French:** *Chat à pieds noirs*

Identification pointers Smallest cat in the region. Two subspecies recognized based on coloration: in north of range pale straw yellow-brown with rusty coloured spots and stripes; in south more reddish-fawn with black spots and stripes. Numerous spots and bars on body, legs, head and tail. Tail short with black rings and tip. Chin and throat white, but 2 or 3 distinct dark bands on throat.

Similar African wild cat larger, longer in leg, no spotting. Genets longer in body and tail.

Habitat Arid to semi-arid scrub and grassland, in generally open terrain, and often in association with termite mounds.

Behaviour Nocturnal, only beginning to forage well after sunset. Usually leaves den well after sunset and returns before sunrise. Solitary, except during mating, and when female is accompanied by cubs. Hunting takes place right through night; foraging distances range from 4.5–16 km. Female home ranges are between 500 ha

and 1 500 ha. Ranges marked by urine spraying, scent marking and scratching.

Food Small rodents most important in diet. Also takes reptiles, amphibians, birds and insects. Male takes prey up to size of Cape hare and bustards.

Reproduction Litter of 1–3 kittens, weighing 78 g average, born after gestation of about 68 days. Most litters born during summer months, but in captivity births recorded throughout year. Female has 1 pair inguinal, 2 pairs abdominal mammae.

Longevity 1–16 years in captivity; 4–8 years in the wild.

Calls Gives vent to loud, throaty *rraaouuh* during mating period, likened to a high-pitched roar; female has soft call to cubs; low growl and spits when annoyed or frightened.

Occurrence Central Kalahari, Nxai Pan (Botswana); Kgalagadi, Augrabies, Namaqua, Karoo, Greater Addo, Mountain Zebra, Willem Pretorius (South Africa).

MEASUREMENTS
Weight: ♂ 1.9 kg (2.5 kg heaviest on record); ♀ 1.3 kg
Shoulder height: 25 cm
Total length: 50–63 cm
Tail length: 16 cm

Right front
24 mm

Right back
22 mm

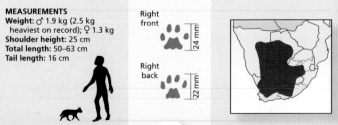

SERVAL

Leptailurus serval

Afrikaans: *Tierboskat* **German:** *Serval* **French:** *Serval*

Identification pointers Slender, long-legged, spotted cat with short tail and large, rounded ears. Body ground colour variable, but usually yellowish-fawn with scattered black spots and bars. Black bars and spots on neck. Black bars extend down legs. Underparts paler, but may be spotted. Back surface of ear has black band, separated from black tip by white patch.

Similar Leopard and cheetah much larger; also both have long tails. Genets smaller, short legs, long tail; exclusively nocturnal.

Habitat Usually areas with water, tall grassland, reed beds and forest fringes. Generally in higher-rainfall areas from sea level to mountain slopes.

Behaviour Often nocturnal, but in protected areas commonly seen during cooler daylight hours. Mainly solitary, but pairs and family groups, of female and young, not unusual. Terrestrial, but agile climbers. Male is territorial; may well apply to females. Home range sizes variable, from 2–30 km². Female home ranges seldom overlap, but that of male may overlap those of 2, or more, females. Follows regularly used pathways and roads when hunting.

Food Small mammals, especially rodents, as well as birds make up bulk of diet. Vlei rats (*Otomys* spp.) particularly important, but also hunts cane-rats and hares.

Reproduction Litter of 1–5 (usually 2–3) cubs, weighing about 200 g, born after gestation of 68–79 days. In the region nearly all recorded births during summer months. Female has 2 pairs abdominal, 1 pair inguinal mammae.

Longevity 13–20 years in captivity; no records in the wild.

Calls Range of snarls, growls and purrs, but seldom heard.

Occurrence Caprivi (Namibia); Chobe, Okavango, Moremi (Botswana); Hwange, Mana Pools, Gonarezhou (Zimbabwe); Banhine, Gorongoza (Mozambique); Kruger, Marakele, iSimangaliso, Ithala, uKhahlamba (South Africa).

MEASUREMENTS
Weight: 8–13 kg
Shoulder height: 60 cm
Total length: 96 cm–1.2 m
Tail length: 25–38 cm

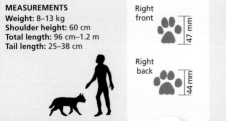

Right front

47 mm

Right back

44 mm

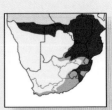

CARACAL

Caracal caracal

Afrikaans: *Rooikat* **German:** *Karakal* **French:** *Caracal*

Identification pointers Robustly built, medium-sized cat; hindquarters higher than shoulders. Long, pointed ears with tuft of longish hair at tips; black-backed, with sprinkling of white hairs. Coat short, dense and soft, ranging from pale yellowish-fawn to rich brick-red. Underparts may be slightly paler to almost white. Prominent black-and-white patches on face, especially around mouth and eyes. Short tail same colour as body.

Similar Cannot be confused with other species in the region.

Habitat Semi-desert to open and woodland savanna, from low- to high-rainfall areas and from sea level to mountain ranges.

Behaviour Mainly nocturnal, but where undisturbed will hunt during cooler daylight hours. Solitary, mainly terrestrial, but can climb well. Male is territorial; home range overlaps those of 1, 2 or more females. Home ranges of females overlap, but contact is probably avoided by olfactory signals. Measured home ranges can be as little as 4 km² to > 100 km², and possibly considerably more in arid areas with a low prey base. They are stalk-crouch-and-pounce hunters.

Food Small to medium-sized mammals, from mice to 40-kg antelope, birds and, rarely, reptiles. In some areas rock hyrax are important in the diet. Considered a major predator of domestic sheep and goats in sheep-farming areas of South Africa and Namibia.

Reproduction Litter of 1–3 kittens, weighing about 250 g, born after gestation of about 79 days. Births may take place any time of year, but there is summer peak in the region. Female has 3 pairs abdominal mammae.

Longevity Up to 17 years in captivity; animals rarely reach 10 years in the wild.

Calls Typical cat-like calls, loud coughs, growls, spitting-hisses, miaows and purrs.

Occurrence In almost all conservation areas within southern Africa.

MEASUREMENTS
Weight: 7–19 kg (♂ heavier than ♀; exceptional ♂ exceeds 30 kg)
Shoulder height: 40–45 cm
Total length: 70 cm–1.1 m
Tail length: 18–34 cm

Right front — 47 mm

Right back — 55 mm

CHEETAH

Acinonyx jubatus

Afrikaans: *Jagluiperd* **German:** *Gepard* **French:** *Guépard*

Identification pointers Often called the 'greyhound' of cats, with its slender body and long legs that are adaptations for high speed. Head small, with short muzzle and clear black line (tear-line) running from inner corner of each eye to corner of mouth. Overall body colour off-white to pale fawn, liberally dotted with more or less uniformly sized rounded black spots. Long tail spotted and black-ringed, usually has white tip.
Similar Leopard has heavier build, with rosettes not spots, no tear-line. Serval smaller.
Habitat Open country, plains, grassland and wooded grassland.
Behaviour Mainly diurnal. Seen singly, in pairs, or in small family parties (female and cubs). Adult males move singly or in small bachelor coalitions of related males. Female establishes territory and drives out other females. Male not as territorial; may move over ranges of several females. Female often has much larger range than male. Relies on rapid (> 70 km/h, may exceed 100 km/h) dashes when hunting,

but only sustained for short distance.
Food Medium-sized mammals, especially antelope up to about 60 kg. Impala, springbok, and young of species such as greater kudu. Hares sometimes taken, as well as birds up to the size of ostrich.
Reproduction 1–5 cubs (usually 3–4), weighing 250–300 g, born after gestation of about 92 days. Births any time of year, but peaks occur in some areas. Female has 4 pairs abdominal/pectoral mammae.
Longevity 17–21 years in captivity; probably 9–12 years in the wild.
Calls *Chirrup* and *churr* contact calls; *nyam nyam* and *ihn ihn* when female calls cubs; growls, snarls, spits and purrs.
Occurrence Khaudom, Etosha (Namibia); Okavango, Central Kalahari, Chobe, Nxai Pan, Makgadikgadi (Botswana); Hwange, Gonarezhou (Zimbabwe); Mapungubwe, Madikwe, Kruger, Pilanesberg, Hluhluwe-Imfolozi, iSimangaliso, Greater Addo, Mountain Zebra (South Africa).

MEASUREMENTS
Weight: 38–72 kg ♂ (most 40–60 kg; ♂ heavier than ♀)
Shoulder height: 80 cm
Total length: 1.6–2.2 m
Tail length: 60–80 cm

Right front

Right back

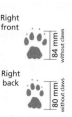

84 mm without claws

80 mm without claws

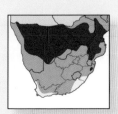

Endangered

LEOPARD

Panthera pardus

Afrikaans: *Luiperd* **German:** *Leopard* **French:** *Léopard*

Identification pointers Powerfully built cat. Colour ranges from off-white to orange-russet; black spots on legs, flanks and head. Spots over rest of body consist of rosettes or broken circles of irregular black spots. Tail about half of total length, white tipped, with rosette spots above; held upward, curved at tip when walking. Ears rounded and white tipped.

Similar Cheetah has slender build, longer legs, solid spots, a black tear-line from eye to mouth. Serval much smaller, with larger, pointed ears, solid spots, shorter tail.

Habitat Coastal plains to mountain ranges, semi-desert to high-rainfall forest.

Behaviour Often nocturnal, but daytime activity is not unusual where not hunted or disturbed. Solitary, except when pair meets in order to mate, or female with cubs. Adult male marks and defends a territory; male's range may overlap those of several females. Terrestrial, but climbs and swims well. Stalk-and-pounce hunter.

Food Wide range of animal food, from insects to large mammals. Most prey small to medium-sized antelope.

Reproduction Litter of 2–3 cubs (only rarely more), weighing about 500 g, born after gestation of about 100 days. Births may take place any time of year. Female has 2 pairs abdominal mammae.

Longevity 21 years in captivity; possibly 9–14 years in the wild.

Calls Commonly heard is territorial 'wood-sawing' call, with 13–16 strokes of a 'saw' in about 12 seconds, repeated every few minutes; growls, purrs, snarls.

Occurrence Namib-Naukluft, Etosha, Khaudom, Caprivi (Namibia); Okavango, Moremi, Chobe, Nxai Pan, Central Kalahari (Botswana); Hwange, Mana Pools, Gonarezhou, Matobo (Zimbabwe); Banhine, Gorongoza (Mozambique); Kgalagadi, Augrabies, Cedarberg, Madikwe, Pilanesberg, Marakele, Mapungubwe, Kruger, Ndumo, uMkhuze, iSimangaliso, Hluhluwe-Imfolozi (South Africa).

MEASUREMENTS
Weight: ♂ 20–90 kg;
♀ 17–60 kg
Shoulder height: 70–80 cm
Total length: 1.6–2.1 m
Tail length: 68 cm–1.1 m

Right front

Right back

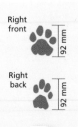

92 mm

92 mm

LION

Panthera leo

Afrikaans: *Leeu* **German:** *Löwe* **French:** *Lion*

Identification pointers Largest cat in the region. Body colour ranges from pale tawny to reddish-grey, with paler underparts. Faint spotting present in cubs, and sometimes retained by adults. Tail same colour as body, with dark brown to black tip tuft. Adult male carries mane of long hair, extending from sides of face onto neck, shoulders and chest.

Similar Unmistakable.

Habitat Desert fringes to woodland and fairly open grassland. Primarily a savanna species.

Behaviour Nocturnal; most hunting is undertaken by lionesses, mainly at night or during cooler daylight hours. Sociable, living in prides of 3–30 individuals. Each pride consists of a stable core of related females, their dependent offspring, and usually a coalition of 2 or more adult males (sometimes just 1). Young males disperse from birth pride and form coalitions. When new males take over a pride they usually kill younger cubs.

Food Mainly medium-sized to large mammals, especially ungulates. Will chase other predators from their kills.

Reproduction 1–4 cubs, weighing about 1.5 kg, born after 110-day gestation. No fixed breeding season. Pride females will suckle any cub. Female has 2 pairs abdominal mammae.

Longevity 30 years in captivity; 13–15 years in the wild.

Calls Roar starts with a few low moans, followed by 4–18 very loud roars, and ends with an average of 15 grunts. Full roars can be heard for up to 8 km. Other calls are commonly associated with social interactions and at kills.

Occurrence Skeleton Coast, Etosha, Khaudom, Caprivi (Namibia); Okavango, Chobe, Central Kalahari, Makgadikgadi, Nxai Pan (Botswana); Hwange, Mana Pools, Gonarezhou (Zimbabwe); Mapungubwe, Marakele, Madikwe, Pilanesberg, Kruger, iSimangaliso, Thembe, Hluhluwe-Imfolozi, Greater Addo (South Africa).

MEASUREMENTS
Weight: ♂ 150–225 kg;
  ♀ 110–152 kg
Shoulder height: ♂ 1.2 m;
  ♀ 1 m
Total length: ♂ 2.5–3.3 m;
  ♀ 2.3–2.7 m
Tail length: 1 m

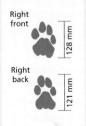

Right front

128 mm

Right back

121 mm

ROCK HYRAX (DASSIE)

Procavia capensis

Afrikaans: *Klipdassie* **German:** *Klippschliefer* **French:** *Daman de rocher*

Identification pointers Small, stoutly built and tailless, with short legs. Overall colour variable, but mainly light to dark brown. Naked gland in centre of back surrounded by longish, black or brown erectile hair. Subspecies Kaokoveld rock dassie (*P.c. welwitschii*) in northern Namibia has white, or yellowish, hair around gland.

Similar Yellow-spotted rock hyrax in northeast of region greyer, with pale yellow dorsal spot. Tree hyrax has very limited range in east and different habitat, with pale to white dorsal spot.

Habitat Mainly mountain and hill ranges, as well as isolated rock outcrops. Has expanded away from these habitats in some areas, sheltering in loose rock piles and in road culverts, as well as burrows dug by other mammals.

Behaviour Diurnal. Lives in colonies of 4–8 individuals (sometimes more), but in prime habitat densities may be very high. Basks in early morning for a lengthy period, then moves off to feed; also basks in evening, especially in cool winter months. Each colony has strict pecking order with dominant male and female. Rarely moves more than a few hundred metres from home shelter. Heavily hunted by larger eagle species, caracal, leopard and human. Populations periodically crash; believed to be linked to disease.

Food Variety of plants, especially leaves, buds and flowers. During drought will eat tree bark.

Reproduction 1–3 (rarely up to 5) young, weighing 150–300 g, born after gestation about 210 days. Young are well developed at birth. Birthing times vary from area to area, but strongly seasonal in each. Female has 1 pair pectoral, 2 pairs inguinal mammae.

Longevity 12 years in captivity; 4–8 years in the wild.

Calls Sharp alarm bark, often ending in a wheeze; chatters and snarls during interactions; cubs chirrup.

Occurrence Common and widespread.

MEASUREMENTS
Weight: 2–5 kg (♂ averages slightly heavier than ♀)
Shoulder height: 15–22 cm
Total length: 40–60 cm

Right front

30 mm

Right back

50 mm

YELLOW-SPOTTED ROCK HYRAX (DASSIE)   *Heterohyrax brucei*

Afrikaans: *Geelkoldassie* **German:** *Buschschliefer* **French:** *Daman de Bruce*

Identification pointers Similar to rock hyrax, but slightly smaller; head narrower and often lighter in colour, but not in all cases. Two subspecies sometimes recognized on basis of coat colour: one more brown, the other more grey, but both with pale dorsal spot. Longish, off-white to yellowish erectile hair around dorsal gland in centre of back. Often has white to pale patch above each eye. Underparts may be slightly paler to dirty white.

Similar Rock hyrax has dark to black dorsal gland hairs; within range often bask together and share rock crevices.

Habitat Mainly mountainous and rocky hill country, including isolated rock outcrops lying on open plains.

Behaviour Mainly diurnal, with most feeding taking place in morning and late afternoon. Climbs readily into trees to feed, as does rock hyrax. Small colonies, but in suitable habitat may live at high densities – 20–53 animals per ha (Matobo in Zimbabwe). Each colonial group consists of a dominant male, females and their young of up to 2 years. Seldom moves as far from shelter as rock hyrax.

Food Predominantly browses; much of the feeding is done in trees and bushes, taking very little grass or low herbage. This contrast to rock hyrax reduces feeding competition between the species.

Reproduction 1–3 (usually 2) young, weighing about 225 g, born after gestation of about > 200 days in March–April in Matobo; this probably applies throughout range in the region. Female has 1 pair pectoral, 2 pairs inguinal mammae.

Longevity > 10 years in captivity; possibly same in the wild.

Calls Shrill alarm bark; male territorial bark-rattle (differs from rock hyrax). Within colony, twitters and chunters.

Occurrence Common within limited range. Mapungubwe, Marakele (South Africa); Mana Pools, Gonarezhou, Matobo (Zimbabwe).

MEASUREMENTS
Weight: 1.3–4.5 kg
Shoulder height: 15–20 cm
Total length: 32–56 cm

Right front

30 mm

Right back

50 mm

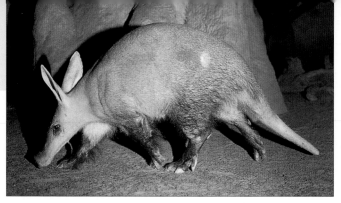

AARDVARK (ANTBEAR)

Oryctéropus afer

Afrikaans: *Erdvark* **German:** *Erdferkel* **French:** *Oryctérope du Cap, Cochon de terre*

Identification pointers Long, pig-like snout, elongated tubular ears, kangaroo-like tail and powerful, stout legs equipped with strong spade-like claws make it unmistakable. Overall colour grey-fawn, often tinged with colour of local soil. Body sparsely covered with coarse, bristle-like hairs, those on base of tail and legs usually darker, to black, in colour. Back distinctly arched; walks with shambling gait.
Similar Should not be mistaken.
Habitat Open woodland, sparse scrub and grassland, but can be expected in most habitats, including forest.
Behaviour Predominantly nocturnal, but sometimes forages during day in cooler hours or periods of severe drought. Nearly always solitary, except when female accompanied by a youngster. Digs extensive burrow systems; occupied ones often characterized by numerous small flies at entrance. When foraging, appears to wander aimlessly until an ant or termite colony is encountered, then tears into it with massively clawed front feet and licks termites and ants out with long, sticky tongue.
Food Mainly ants and termites.
Reproduction Single young, weighing about 2 kg, born after gestation of about 210 days. Pregnant females and presence of young recorded for most months, with probable peak during rains. Female has 1 pair inguinal, 1 pair abdominal mammae.
Longevity 18–24 years in captivity; nothing known for wild, but probably less.
Calls Subdued grunts and snuffles when foraging; calf-like bellow if frightened or injured.
Occurrence Etosha, Khaudom, Waterberg, Caprivi (Namibia); Okavango, Chobe, Nxai Pan, Central Kalahari (Botswana); Hwange, Mana Pools, Gonarezhou (Zimbabwe); Banhine, Gorongoza (Mozambique); Kgalagadi, Augrabies, West Coast, Agulhas, Karoo, Greater Addo, Pilanesberg, Madikwe, Marakele, Mapungubwe, Kruger, Golden Gate, Willem Pretorius, Ithala, iSimangaliso, Hluhluwe-Imfolozi (South Africa).

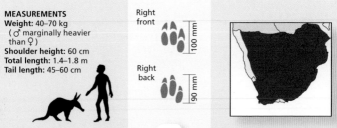

MEASUREMENTS
Weight: 40–70 kg
(♂ marginally heavier than ♀)
Shoulder height: 60 cm
Total length: 1.4–1.8 m
Tail length: 45–60 cm

Right front
100 mm

Right back
90 mm

GROUND PANGOLIN

Manis temmincki

Afrikaans: *Ietermagô* **German:** *Steppenschuppentier* **French:** *Pangolin terrestre du Cap*

Identification pointers Back, sides and tail covered with large scales. Curls into ball to protect unscaled underparts if frightened. Tiny, pointed head, without teeth. Powerfully developed hind legs and tail. Small forelegs used for digging out prey, rarely for walking.

Similar No similar species in the region.

Habitat Favours dry woodland savanna, but also in open scrub, grassland and semi-desert; in areas with annual rainfall of 250–1 400 mm. Does not occur south of Orange (Gariep) River in South Africa, possibly because cold winters drive their main ant prey deep underground.

Behaviour Predominantly nocturnal, but with some crepuscular activity. Will forage during day when overcast or during severe drought, when prey access is more restricted. May excavate its own burrow, but usually occupies those dug by other species. Burrows may be closed from inside when occupied. Solitary, except when a female is with her single young, which clings to her back at base of tail when she is foraging. Each animal has several burrows, or lies up in dense vegetation, within a fixed home range of 10–1 100 ha; size probably dictated by food availability.

Food Certain species of ants and termites, their eggs and larvae.

Reproduction Single young, weighing 330–450 g, born after gestation of about 140 days. Birthing season unclear, but meagre records indicate mainly winter months in the region. Female has 1 pair pectoral mammae.

Longevity No records; rarely survives long in captivity.

Calls Generally silent, but makes snuffling noises when foraging.

Occurrence Etosha, Khaudom, Caprivi, Waterberg (Namibia); Okavango, Chobe, Central Kalahari (Botswana); Hwange, Mana Pools, Gonarezhou (Zimbabwe); Kgalagadi, Pilanesberg, Madikwe, Mapungubwe, Kruger (South Africa).

MEASUREMENTS
Weight: 5–18 kg
(rarely > 16 kg)
Total length: 70 cm–1.4 m
(rarely > 1.2 m)
Tail length: 30–45 cm

Right back

60 mm

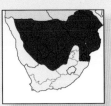

Endangered

91

FOUR-TOED SENGI (ELEPHANT SHREW) *Petrodromus tetradactylus*

Afrikaans: *Viertoonklaasneus* **German:** *Vierzehenrüsselratte* **French:** *Pétrodrome à quatre orteils*

Identification pointers A large sengi, also known misleadingly as elephant shrew. Hind legs and feet considerably longer than front. Long, slender and mobile snout, and fairly long, membranous ears. Coat is soft and dense, buff-coloured above with a slight orange or reddish-brown tinge. Underparts are whitish, often with yellow or orange tinge on flanks. White ring around large eye.

Similar Considerably larger than other 8 sengis in the region; only marginally overlaps range of 3 other species, but largely separated on habitat requirements. Trunk-like snout ('flute snoot') separates it from any equal-sized rodents in range.

Habitat Areas with dense vegetation, including thickets around rock outcrops, closed woodland, riverine forest, as well as drier coastal forest.

Behaviour Active at night, but also during morning and late afternoon. Pairs probably occupy and defend overlapping territories against intruders, male seeing off males, female seeing off females. Each territory (size not known in the region, in Kenya averages 1.2 ha) has a network of paths that is patrolled regularly and kept clear of debris such as leaves. Pathways have bare patches every 40–100 cm resulting from sengis' bounding gait.

Food Mainly insects, including termites and ants.

Reproduction Single (rarely 2) young, weighing about 32 g, born after gestation of about 60 days. As with all sengi young, well developed at birth and soon move around. Meagre records in the region indicate main birthing August–October, but possibly all months. Female has 1 pair pectoral, 2 pairs abdominal mammae.

Longevity A captive lived for 6 years 7 months.

Calls Shrill squeak; drums on ground with hind feet and tail.

Occurrence Fairly common within its limited local range. Ndumo, Phinda, Thembe, iSimangaliso, Kruger (South Africa).

MEASUREMENTS
Weight: 160–280 g
Total length: 35 cm
Tail length: 16 cm

Right front — 26 mm

Right back — 60 mm

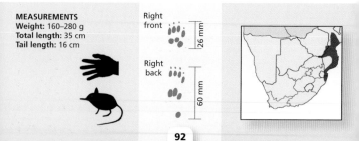

ROUND-EARED SENGI (ELEPHANT SHREW)

Macroscelides proboscideus

Afrikaans: *Rondeoorklaasneus* **German:** *Kurzohrrüsselspringer* **French:** *Macroscélide à oreilles courtes*

Identification pointers Distinctive trunk-like snout. Ears more rounded and broader than those of other species. Lacks white eye-ring of other sengis. Over much of southern range buffy-grey (some more brown) with white to off-white underparts; animals from northern part paler, in Namib Desert creamy-buff with pale coloured tail. May consist of a complex of at least 3 species.

Similar Bushveld sengi in north of its range; longer ears and a white eye-ring.

Habitat Open country where there is low scrub and sparse grass cover; substrate may be sandy or gravel plains.

Behaviour Active during early morning and late afternoon, with nocturnal activity. On cool, overcast days may be seen foraging at any time. Usually seen singly, but probably live as pairs either in overlapping, or mutual, territories. Efficient burrower, but readily shelters under rocks and in dense vegetation; latter seems to serve more as emergency retreat. Normally hunts from

shade cover, dashing out to retrieve prey and then rushing back. In cold conditions remains in shelter in a state of torpor; basks at burrow entrance during cooler hours.

Food Omnivore that feeds on various insects, but leaves and seeds constitute more than 50% of diet in some areas.

Reproduction 2 (or less commonly 1) well-developed young, weighing 6–8 g, born after gestation of about 64 days. Birthing throughout year, but with decline in summer; may be regional differences. Female has 1 pair pectoral, 2 pairs abdominal mammae.

Longevity A captive lived just over 6 years.

Calls Squeals when handled; drums ground rapidly with hind feet.

Occurrence Restricted to west but common over much of range. Skeleton Coast, Namib-Naukluft, Fish River (Namibia); Richtersveld, Augrabies, Namaqua, Tankwa, Karoo, Greater Addo, Camdeboo (South Africa).

MEASUREMENTS
Weight: 31–47 g
Total length: 23 cm
Tail length: 12 cm

Right front
7 mm

Right back
16 mm

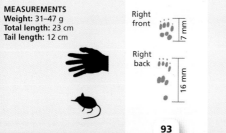

BUSHVELD SENGI (ELEPHANT SHREW) *Elephantulus intufi*

Afrikaans: *Bosveldklaasneus* **German:** *Trockenland-Elefantenspitzmaus* **French:** *Rat à trompe jaune*

Identification pointers Typical sengi, with elongated, tubular snout and fairly long ears. Back feet considerably longer than front feet. Overall body colour varies in range: straw-buff heavily grizzled with black hairs in east; pale straw-buff with less obvious grizzling in west; northern-most animals more grey. All have very pale to white underparts and conspicuous ring of short, white hairs around eyes.

Similar Round-eared sengi has shorter, rounded ears; shares part of range, but usually in more open terrain. Western rock sengi also in much of Namibian range, but in rocky habitat.

Habitat Areas with annual rainfall between 150 mm and < 450 mm; avoids totally open areas but even meagre scrub cover suffices. Usually on sandy soils.

Behaviour Diurnal and nocturnal, with most foraging taking place at dawn and dusk. A monogamous pair share home range or occupy overlapping ones. Animals in some areas dig burrows at base of low bushes or grass tussocks, those in other areas have dens, not burrows, at base of dense bushes or in rock piles. Makes use of regularly used trails between shelter; usually hunts from shade during day, rarely hunts in areas without cover.

Food Insects, especially ants; larger prey carried back to bush shelters.

Reproduction 1–3 (usually 2) well-developed young, weighing about 8 g, born after gestation of about 56 days. In some areas birthing August–March, but probably breeds all year in Namibia. Female has 1 pair inguinal, 2 pairs abdominal mammae.

Longevity 1 captive > 8 years.

Calls High-pitched squeak; foot-drumming at different tempos common.

Occurrence Largely restricted to Namibia, southern Botswana, and marginally in adjacent areas of South Africa. Etosha, Skeleton Coast, Namib-Naukluft (Namibia); Central Kalahari (Botswana); Mapungubwe, Kgalagadi, Augrabies (South Africa).

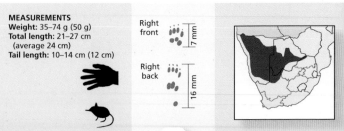

MEASUREMENTS
Weight: 35–74 g (50 g)
Total length: 21–27 cm
(average 24 cm)
Tail length: 10–14 cm (12 cm)

Right front | 7 mm

Right back | 16 mm

WESTERN ROCK SENGI (ELEPHANT SHREW)

Elephantulus rupestris

Afrikaans: *Westelike klipklasneus* **German:** *Westliche Klippen-Elefantenspitzmaus*
French: *Rat à trompe des rochers de l'ouest*

Identification pointers There are 7 species of sengi in genus *Elephantulus* within the region: 4 overlap range of this species, 2 can be found in same habitat. Difficult to separate in field, but other 2 only occur in south of range. In south yellowish-brown, strongly 'pencilled' with black, with broad patch of rufous-yellow at base of each ear. Flanks and underparts greyish-white; whitish rings around eyes. Animals in Namibia much paler.
Similar Eastern rock sengi only overlaps slightly in southeast. Cape rock sengi and Karoo rock sengi overlap slightly in south. Similar-coloured rodents in area lack trunk-like snout.
Habitat Rock outcrops, boulder piles and broken hill ranges.
Behaviour Mainly diurnal, but also active at night. Foraging is solitary and takes place throughout day, interspersed with rest periods. Stays in shade, dashing out periodically to snatch up insects, which are carried back and eaten in shade. Basks in early mornings, especially after cold nights. Does not emerge during very cold spells, going into a state of torpor.
Food Insects, especially ants and termites, constitute as much as 90% of diet.
Reproduction 1–2 well-developed young, weighing 9–10 g, born after gestation of about 56 days. Most births coincide with rains, September–April, but young have been recorded in other months. Female has 1 pair pectoral, 2 pairs abdominal mammae.
Longevity No records for this species, but a similar-sized bushveld sengi lived > 8 years
Calls Series of high-pitched squeaks; hind foot drumming is common to all sengis.
Occurrence Namib-Naukluft, Fish River (Namibia); Richtersveld, Augrabies, Mokala, Mountain Zebra, Camdeboo, Greater Addo (South Africa).

MEASUREMENTS
Weight: 54–78 g
(average 65 g)
Total length: 28 cm
Tail length: 15 cm

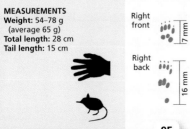

Right
front

7 mm

Right
back

16 mm

SOUTHERN AFRICAN HEDGEHOG

Atelerix frontalis

Afrikaans: *Krimpvarkie* **German:** *Südafrikanischer Igel* **French:** *Hérisson d'Afrique du Sud*

Identification pointers Upperparts covered with short, but strong, sharp spines extending from forehead, over back to rump. Spines white at base and tip, with dark brown or black band in between. Face, legs and tail covered in dark to grey-brown hair; underparts off-white to black. Prominent white band of hair across forehead to beyond ear base; sometimes a white spot below each eye. Tail short, but not visible; legs relatively long; ears prominent and rounded.

Similar Porcupine much bigger, with long quills and spines, tiny rounded ears.

Habitat Wide variety, excluding true desert and high-rainfall areas. Only known where annual rainfall < 800 mm.

Behaviour Nocturnal, but will wander about during day in rainy season. Lies up during day among dry vegetation and in burrows dug by other species. Fixed resting places are only used by females with young, or during hibernation in cooler months (May–July). Solitary, except female accompanied by young. Excellent senses of smell and hearing, but sight poor. When threatened, curls into a tight ball with spines protecting head and underparts.

Food Insects, millipedes, earthworms, mice, lizards, fungi and some fruit.

Reproduction 1–9 young (average 4), weighing 9–11 g, born after gestation of about 35 days. In sixth week grows hardened spines and begins to forage with mother. Most births in warm, wet summer months; female may have several litters in a season. Female has 2 pairs pectoral, 1 pair abdominal mammae, occasionally more.

Longevity 3–7 years in captivity; same in the wild.

Calls Snuffles, snorts, growls when foraging, or individuals meet; alarm call a high-pitched scream.

Occurrence Etosha, Waterberg (Namibia); Hwange (Zimbabwe); Mapungubwe, Kruger, Madikwe, Pilanesberg, Mountain Zebra, Camdeboo, Greater Addo (South Africa).

MEASUREMENTS
Weight: 230–480 g (average 400 g) (♂ averages heavier than ♀)
Total length: 20 cm
Tail length: 2 cm

Right front

26 mm without claws

Right back

26 mm without claws

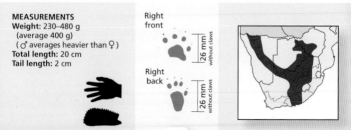

WHITE-TOOTHED (MUSK) SHREWS

Crocidura spp.

Afrikaans: *Muskusskeerbekke* **German:** *Weißzahnspitzmäuse* **French:** *Crocidure*

Identification pointers 17 species of shrew in the region; 9 are white-toothed shrews. Very similar, but all identifiable as shrews. White-toothed shrews small, mouse-sized, with long, wedge-shaped snouts and short legs. Short, soft coats may be grey, black, fawn or brown. Sparse, long bristles on tail. Teeth wholly white.

Similar Forest shrews (*Myosorex* spp.); 4 species; lack long hairs on tail. The 3 dwarf shrews (*Suncus* spp.) have long hairs on tails, difficult to separate from smallest white-toothed shrews. Can be confused with some of the smallest rodents.

Habitat Virtually all habitats, from swamps to high mountains, coastal dunes to forest, deserts to high-rainfall areas. More than one species may be found in any area.

Behaviour Alternating periods of activity and rest throughout a 24-hour period. The few species that have been studied mark and defend fixed home ranges. Mainly solitary, but may occur at high densities in most suitable habitats. Some live in short burrows; others construct domed nests in dense vegetation. Use same pathways, which radiate from den, when foraging.

Food Insects, also range of other invertebrates, such as earthworms, snails and spiders. Larger species will also tackle young mice and small lizards.

Reproduction Litter of 2–6 naked, helpless young, weighing as little as 1 g, born after gestation of about 18 days. Births possibly any time of year, with seasonal peaks; female may have several litters. Female (all species) has 3 pairs inguinal mammae.

Longevity As little as 16–18 months in the wild.

Calls Twittering when foraging; sharp squeaks when alarmed, or in conflict situations.

Occurrence A few species very localized, but others widespread and common. One, or more, species in virtually every conservation area in the region.

MEASUREMENTS
Weight: 6–45 g
Total length: 10–22 cm
Tail length: 3–9 cm
  (tail usually < half total length)

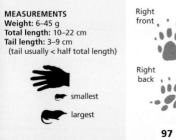

smallest

largest

Right front

6–12 mm

Right back

11–21 mm

97

GOLDEN MOLES

Family Chrysochloridae

Afrikaans: *Gouemolle* **German:** *Goldmulle* **French:** *Taupes dorées*

Identification pointers: Eighteen species in the region; all very similar and difficult to separate without detailed examination of dentition and DNA. Lacks visible eyes, external ears and visible tail. Soft, glossy coat ranges from silvery-white to deep chocolate-brown and black, but most are some shade of brown. Two long, strong claws on front feet. Rubbery nose-pad.

Similar Rodent moles (mole-rats) have tiny but visible eyes, tiny exposed ear-openings, 2 pairs very large incisor teeth, short, flattened tails and 3 strong, long claws on each front foot.

Habitat Sand dunes of Namib Desert, to high-altitude grassland and moist forest. Most species associated with sandy soils, but a few found in clay or loamy soils; none can cope with heavy clay.

Behaviour Spend much of their lives underground, although a few (such as Grant's) quite often forage on surface. Surface foragers do so at night, but others may be active at any time. All species have

deeper-running, permanent tunnels, as well as foraging tunnels that meander close to surface and frequently cause visible soil disturbance. At least 2 species push mounds like mole-rats. Little known about social structure.

Food Insects and other invertebrates, including earthworms; some take small reptiles.

Reproduction Litter of 1–2 young, born naked and helpless. Newborns of *Amblysomus* spp. weigh about 5 g. Some species breed in wet season, when food abundant; others during cooler, drier months; others, perhaps most, have litters any time of year. Female has 1 pair abdominal, 1 pair inguinal mammae.

Longevity No records.

Calls Sharp squeaks when handled.

Occurrence Widely in conservation areas within South Africa; only one species in Namibia restricted to Namib-Naukluft; none occur in Botswana; 2 marginally in far eastern Zimbabwe.

MEASUREMENTS
Weight: 16–538 g
Total length: 7–23 cm

smallest

largest

STRAW-COLOURED FRUIT-BAT

Eidolon helvum

Afrikaans: *Geelvrugtevlermuis* **German:** *Palmenflughund* **French:** Rousette des palmiers

Identification pointers Largest bat in the region. Dog-like face, large, reddish-brown eyes and prominent rounded ears. Wings long and tapered, dark brown to black in colour. Body colour varies from dull yellow/grey-brown to rich yellowish-brown, with paler underparts. Hindquarters and limbs usually darker than rest of body. Tail very short.

Similar Egyptian fruit-bat smaller, dull dark brown to greyish-brown. Epauletted fruit-bats have distinctive white hair tufts at ear bases and on shoulders.

Habitat Mainly tropical forest species, but disperses as far south as this region and can be expected anywhere, but less frequently in arid west.

Behaviour Nocturnal; searches for food after sunset, may fly several kilometres seeking fruiting trees. In this area usually encountered singly or in small groups, but in tropics may form colonies of hundreds of thousands, even millions. Nearest known large colonies in northeastern Zambia and central Mozambique. Even in large colonies will cluster in groups of 10–50 individuals. Roosts are noisy and smelly; animals jockey for prime locations. Little known in the region.

Food Wide range of both wild and cultivated fruit.

Reproduction Not known to breed in region. In tropical breeding grounds, a single young (very rarely twins), weighing 40–50 g, born after gestation of 120 days. Up to 6 weeks of age young is carried by mother to and from feeding grounds. Female has 1 pair pectoral mammae.

Longevity A captive lived > 21 years.

Calls Squeals, screams and chattering at roost; usually quiet in flight. Noise levels can be extreme in large colonies but no such colonies in the region as far as known.

Occurrence A migrant from the tropics that can turn up anywhere, from Namib Desert to subtropical KwaZulu-Natal. Authors have recorded it in Namib Desert, Great Karoo and coastal KwaZulu-Natal.

MEASUREMENTS
Weight: 230–350 g
Wingspan: 75 cm
Forearm: 11.5 cm
Total length: 19 cm
Tail length: 4–20 cm

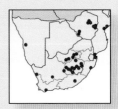

WAHLBERG'S EPAULETTED FRUIT-BAT *Epomophorus wahlbergi*

Afrikaans: *Wahlberg-witkolvrugtevlermuis* **German:** *Wahlberg-Epaulettenflughund*
French: *Épomophores*

Identification pointers Eight fruit-bat species occur in the region; 4 are epauletted fruit-bats, of which only 2 are common. Wahlberg's and Peters's have fox-like heads and white tufts of hair at base of ears. Male has white-haired shoulder pockets – epaulettes that give group name; white hair prominent when pouch is spread. Overall body colour varies from light to dark brown.
Similar Other 2 epauletted fruit-bats very rare, not present in range of Wahlberg's and Peters's. Egyptian fruit-bat occurs over range of Wahlberg's, but plain in colour; roosts in caves and not trees.
Habitat Forest and riverine woodland, but will extend into drier woodland. Sometimes forms roost in towns.
Behaviour Nocturnal; leaves roost after sunset and may fly several kilometres to feeding grounds. May search locally for seasonally fruiting trees. Roosts in small numbers, up to a few hundred, in trees and bushes; will roost under open roofs

of buildings. Much squabbling within colony, with each animal keeping a specific distance from its neighbours.
Food Soft wild and cultivated fruit; feeds on tree flowers for nectar.
Reproduction Single (very rarely 2) young, weighing about 20 g, born after gestation of some 105 days. Births mainly linked to summer rainy season (November–January). Female has 1 pair pectoral mammae.
Longevity Not known.
Calls Squeaks, chuckles; male makes repetitive sharp metallic, or clinking, call (miniature hammer on tin can).
Occurrence Wahlberg's and Peters's occur along coastal belt in south and east; Wahlberg's extends inland, mainly on river courses; Peters's more extensive inland. **Wahlberg's:** Garden Route, Greater Addo, iSimangaliso, Kruger (South Africa). **Peters's:** Kruger (South Africa); Gonarezhou, Mana Pools (Zimbabwe); Chobe, Moremi, Okavango (Botswana).

MEASUREMENTS
Weight: 70–160 g
Wingspan: 50 cm
Forearm: 8.4 cm
Total length: 14 cm

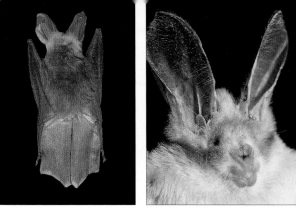

SLIT-FACED BATS

Nycteris spp.

Afrikaans: *Spleetneusvlermuise* **German:** *Schlitznasen* **French:** *Nyctères*

Identification pointers Five species in the region, of which just one (Egyptian slit-faced bat *N. thebaica*) is common and widespread. Very long, round-tipped ears; split running down length of face. Long tail, forked at tip; wings are rounded. Fur on upperparts usually light to dark brown (occasionally reddish-orange); underparts pale brown to dirty white.

Similar Long-eared bats (*Laephotis* spp.), of which 3 species in the region, much smaller, ears stand out at angle to head, whereas those of the slit-faced are vertical and parallel. Long-eared bats are rare and have limited ranges.

Habitat Wide-ranging Egyptian slit-faced occupies virtually all habitats; 2 species occur in riverine woodland; the other 3 species have very limited southern African ranges.

Behaviour Commonly solitary, or hanging in pairs. Most species roost in small numbers, in caves, buildings and in trees and bushes. Egyptian slit-faced bat may gather in hundreds. All slow but highly efficient fliers. Most prey is taken on the wing; will also snatch invertebrates off the ground. Larger prey taken to a regularly used perch to eat. Perches identifiable by accumulations of non-edible parts such as moth wings.

Food Insects and other invertebrates, but large slit-faced bat (*N. grandis*) – known only from eastern Zimbabwe – also takes small fish and frogs.

Reproduction Single young, weighing about 6 g, born after gestation of about 150 days (Egyptian, probably similar for other species). Female carries young with her initially on feeding forays. Birthing usually during summer rains. Female has 1 pair pectoral mammae.

Longevity Unknown.

Calls High-frequency calls very rarely heard by humans.

Occurrence Only Egyptian slit-faced common and widespread, occurs in many conservation areas; others have very limited local range and little is known about them.

MEASUREMENTS
Weight: 11–40 g
Wingspan: 24–35 cm
Forearm: 3.8–6.5 cm
Total length: 9–16 cm

smallest

largest

HORSESHOE BATS

Rhinolophus spp.

Afrikaans: *Saalneusvlermuise* **German:** *Hufeisennasen* **French:** *Rhinolophes*

Identification pointers At least 14 species of horseshoe bat occur in the region, all easily recognizable as such, but difficult to identify to species level. All characterized by elaborate nose-leaves over face between mouth and forehead. Squared tails; quite large ears lack a tragus (skin extension). Colour varies between species and sometimes within single species, but most are various shades of brown or grey-brown, with usually paler underparts.

Similar Leaf-nosed bats (*Hipposideros* spp.), but they have different and less elaborate nose-leaves.

Habitat Savanna woodland, but in most habitats, extending from desert to high-rainfall montane areas.

Behaviour Some species roost in small numbers; others, such as Geoffroy's, may come together in thousands. Principally roost in caves, but mine shafts and dark corners of buildings also used. Hang free by their feet, singly or in well-spaced groups, with wings enfolding the body.

Most other insect-eating bats roost with wings folded at sides. Broad, round-tipped wings allow for slow, butterfly-like flight. Most, if not all, have hunting territories.

Food Generally low-flying hunters; take wide range of flying insects such as moths and beetles, but some species will snatch invertebrates off the ground.

Reproduction Single young (very rarely twins), weighing about 25% of adult body weight, born after gestation of 90–120 days (as in most bats, involves delayed implantation, or slowed development). Most births coincide with summer months. At least in some, young are left at roost when mother forages at night. Female has 1 pair pectoral mammae.

Longevity No records in the region; a European horseshoe bat (*R. ferrumequinum*) lived for at least 24 years.

Calls At frequencies rarely audible to human ears.

Occurrence Absent only from the Kalahari in Botswana.

MEASUREMENTS
Weight: 4–27 g
Wingspan: 20–40 cm
Forearm: 4.2–6.5 cm
Total length: 7–11 cm

smallest

largest

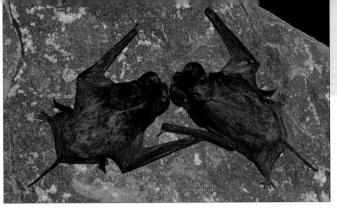

EGYPTIAN FREE-TAILED BAT

Tadarida aegyptiaca

Afrikaans: *Egiptiese losstertvlermuis* **German:** *Ägyptische Bulldoggfledermaus* **French:** *Tadaride d'Égypt*

Identification pointers Region has 14 species of free-tailed bat, but only Egyptian free tailed is widespread and common. All easily identified as free-tails, but separation at species level extremely difficult. Tail is free and only half, or less, enclosed by narrow interfemoral membrane. Also known as bulldog, mastiff or wrinkle-lipped bats, for dog-like faces and wrinkled upper lip. Coat hair short and velvety in shades of brown to blackish. Wings usually narrow and long.

Similar In hand should not be confused with any other bat group because of partly free tail and wrinkled lips.

Habitat One or more species occupy most habitats. Favours open woodland and river courses; also semi-arid and high-rainfall areas. Egyptian occurs in most drier habitats.

Behaviour May roost in hundreds in caves, rock crevices, hollow trees and behind loose bark of dead trees. Substantial colonies formed in buildings. Unlike most other bats, can scuttle rapidly along ground. When hunting, they tend to fly high and rapidly.

Food Wide range of insects, including moths and beetles. The authors have watched these bats on the ground snatching emerging termite alates.

Reproduction Despite abundance, very little known. Single young, weighing about 25% of adult body weight, born after gestation of about 120 days. Births in summer months. Young are left at roost and not carried by female when foraging. Female has 1 pair pectoral mammae.

Longevity No African records exist. A South American species known to live up to 8 years.

Calls High-frequency chitter; more easily picked up by human ear than those of many other insect-eating bats.

Occurrence This species common and widespread throughout the region; many other species rare, or with limited distribution. In many conservation areas.

MEASUREMENTS
Weight: 15 g
Wingspan: 30 cm
Forearm: 4.8 cm
Total length: 11 cm
Tail length: 3.8 cm

SOUTHERN AFRICAN SPRINGHARE

Pedetes capensis

Afrikaans: *Springhaas* **German:** *Springhase* **French:** *Lièvre sauteur*

Identification pointers A true rodent, not a hare. Resembles small wallaby, with long and well-developed hind legs and hopping gait. Forelegs very short, used only for digging out food and excavating burrows. Tail long, bushy and black towards tip. Ears quite long; eyes noticeably large. Upperparts yellowish- or reddish-fawn; underparts paler to white.

Similar See true hares; they move on all 4 feet, have much longer ears, and short, black-and-white tails.

Habitat Compacted sandy soils with short vegetation, mainly semi-arid areas.

Behaviour Nocturnal, terrestrial and not territorial. Burrow occupied by single animal, or female and young; several burrows may be in close proximity. Digs 2 types of burrow: sloping with considerable amounts of sand around entrance; and vertical, clean escape burrow. Occupied burrows often blocked with sand from inside. Can occur in large numbers in areas of prime habitat.

Food Grass, grass roots and other plants, as well as cultivated crops.

Reproduction Single (very rarely 2) well-developed young, weighing about 300 g, born after gestation of 72–82 days. Young remains in burrow for first 6–7 weeks of life. In some areas births seasonal, but in others almost throughout year. Female has 1 pair pectoral mammae.

Longevity 8 years in captivity.

Calls Normally silent, but gives soft grunts on feeding grounds; harsh, loud scream if caught.

Occurrence Widespread and common despite heavy hunting pressure by humans in some areas. Etosha, Namib-Naukluft, Khaudom (Namibia); Chobe, Okavango, Central Kalahari, Nxai Pan, Makgadikgadi (Botswana); Hwange, Gonarezhou (Zimbabwe); Mapungubwe, Kruger, Marakele, Madikwe, Pilanesberg, Mokala, Kgalagadi, Augrabies, Willem Pretorius, Mountain Zebra, Camdeboo, Greater Addo (South Africa).

MEASUREMENTS
Weight: 2.5–3.8 kg
Total length: 75–85 cm
Tail length: 35–45 cm

Left back   Right back

38 mm

CAPE (SOUTHERN) PORCUPINE

Hystrix africaeaustralis

Afrikaans: *Ystervark* **German:** *Südafrikanisches Stachelschwein* **French:** *Porc-épic du Cap*

Identification pointers Large size and long, black-and-white banded quills and spines diagnostic. Flanks, neck, head and underparts have dark, coarse hair. Crest of long, erectile, coarse hair runs from top of head to shoulders. Crest, quills and spines raised when animal alarmed. Ears small and rounded; eyes small.

Similar Southern African hedgehog much smaller, with short quills; rolls into defensive ball.

Habitat Prefers broken, rocky country, although occurs in virtually all habitats.

Behaviour Strictly nocturnal, spending day in burrows (self-excavated, or taken over from other species), or in rock crevices, caves and even among dense vegetation. A feature of regularly used porcupine dens is an accumulation of bones, gnawed to prevent overgrowth of incisors and as source of calcium. Regularly used pathways in home range typically show signs of foraging, as well as occasional cast quills and cigar-shaped droppings. Several porcupines may share a den, but foraging usually a solitary activity. Male and female form monogamous pair.

Food Roots, bulbs, corms, tubers and tree bark favoured; also eats some wild fruit and cultivated crops.

Reproduction Litter of 1–4 (usually 1–2) well-developed young, weighing 100–300 g (up to 450 g unusual), born after gestation of about 94 days. Quills harden in second week. In some areas, young born at any time of year, in others births are seasonal. Female has 2 pairs pectoral mammae, pointing to sides.

Longevity At least 20 years in captivity; 12–15 years in the wild.

Calls When alarmed, rattles hollow tail quills and stamps hind feet; soft grunts and snuffles when foraging, or when 2 or more animals meet.

Occurrence Absent only from Namib Desert. Present in virtually all conservation areas in the region.

MEASUREMENTS
Weight: 10–24 kg
Shoulder height: 25 cm
(> 45 cm when quills raised)
Total length: 75 cm–1 m
Tail length: 10–15 cm
(excluding quills)

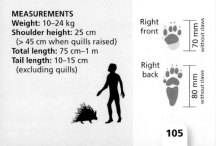

Right front — 70 mm without claws

Right back — 80 mm without claws

GREATER CANE-RAT

Thryonomys swinderianus

Afrikaans: *Grootrietrot* **German:** *Große Rohrratte* **French:** *Grand aulacode*

Identification pointers Large, coarse-haired, stockily built rodent with short tail. Upperparts and sides generally dark speckled brown; underparts range from off-white to greyish-brown. Body hair falls out easily if animal handled.

Similar Lesser cane-rat similar but smaller; limited range in Zimbabwe, usually in drier habitats.

Habitat Reed beds and dense vegetation near water.

Behaviour Nocturnal and crepuscular. Dens up in dense vegetation cover, or burrows among reed beds. Tends to forage alone, but lives in loosely associated groups of up to 8 or 10 animals. Within feeding areas forms distinct runs, characterized by small piles of cut grass or reed segments along their length. Excellent swimmer; sometimes swims between feeding grounds. Rarely moves more than 50 m from habitat.

Food Roots, leaves, stems and shoots of grasses, reeds and sedges. A pest in sugar-cane growing areas.

Reproduction Litter of 4 (up to 8) well-developed young, weighing 80–190 g (average 117 g), born after gestation of 137–172 days (average 154 days). Most births during summer rainy season. Young born in hollow or burrow, lined with grass and leaves. Female has 3 pairs pectoral/abdominal mammae, protruding on sides.

Longevity Only record is for captive that lived 4 years 4 months.

Calls Snorts and snuffles when foraging; stamping of hind feet on ground when alarmed; sharp alarm whistle and a booming grunt.

Occurrence Restricted to east of region, wherever there is suitable habitat. Despite being hunted, still fairly common. Okavango, Moremi, Chobe (Botswana); Mana Pools, Gonarezhou (Zimbabwe); Gorongoza (Mozambique); Mapungubwe, Marakele, Kruger, iSimangaliso, Ndumo, uMkhuze, Hluhluwe-Imfolozi, Oribi Gorge, Great Fish (South Africa).

MEASUREMENTS
Weight: 3–5 kg (♂ averages 20–25% heavier than ♀)
Total length: 65–80 cm
Tail length: 15–20 cm

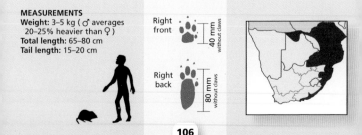

Right front
40 mm without claws

Right back
80 mm without claws

RODENT MOLES (MOLE-RATS)

Family Bathyergidae

Afrikaans: *Tandmolle* **German:** *Sandgräber* **French:** *Rats-taupes*

Identification pointers Six species occur in the region; all similar but differ in detail. All characterized by plump appearance, soft fur, 2 very large pairs of incisor teeth, short and flattened tail, and tiny eyes and ears. Snout is pig-like; long, strong claws on front feet; legs short.

Similar Golden moles, but they lack visible eyes or ear openings; just 2 large claws on front foot, and no tail; most species push surface tunnels, although at least 2 largest species also push earth mounds.

Habitat Sandy soils, but at least common mole-rat (*Cryptomys hottentotus*) also in different soils, including on broken hill- and mountain-slopes. All avoid heavy clay soils. Some occupy desert, and semi-desert sands in Namib, Botswana and northwest South Africa.

Behaviour Nocturnal and diurnal. Fossorial, spend most of lives underground, and dig extensive networks of burrows that are marked on surface by mounds of excavated earth. Most digging activity is triggered by rain; dig with snout, teeth and front feet. Within burrow systems there are chambers for food storage and for dropping young. All species have complex social system, but highly evolved in Damara mole-rat (*Cryptomys damarensis*), with dominant reproductive pair controlling a colony.

Food Roots, bulbs and tubers.

Reproduction Litter size varies by species with Damara having 2–3 pups, Cape mole-rat 4–10. Gestation of largest (Cape dune mole-rat) about 60–75 days and pups weigh some 34 g; Namaqua dune mole-rat > 52 days. Smaller *Cryptomys* (4 spp.) pups weigh < 10 g. Appear to be seasonal breeders.

Longevity Cape mole-rat up to 3 years; a common mole-rat lived in captivity 9 years 7 months.

Calls Foot-drumming in tunnels; squeaks, grunts, growls.

Occurrence 3 species occur only in South Africa; all common to abundant. In many conservation areas through ranges.

MEASUREMENTS
Weight: 100–890 g
Total length: 15–32 cm
Tail length: 2–5 cm

smallest

largest

DASSIE RAT (NOKI)

Petromus typicus

Afrikaans: *Dassierot* **German:** *Felsenratte* **French:** *Rat des rochers africain, Noki*

Identification pointers Squirrel-like, although tail is hairy, not bushy. Grizzled grey-brown to brown with hindquarters usually more uniformly brown. Underparts off-white to yellowish-brown. Head somewhat flattened and ears small, rounded and dark in colour.
Similar See dormice; rock dormouse (*Graphiurus platyops*) shares western range, but much smaller, with bushy tail and overall grey colour. Larger rock hyrax has no tail.
Habitat Rocky areas in arid to semi-arid areas. Usually areas with < 300 mm annual rainfall.
Behaviour Monogamous pairs, or family groups, occupy rock crevices and defend fixed home range. Active by day, although much activity restricted to early morning and late afternoon, especially through summer. Moves about in shade during hottest hours. Often observed basking in early morning sun. Plucks off leaf or twig and feeds in shade. Urinates and defecates at midden sites, which become stained yellowish-white. Can reach densities of 15 animals to 6 ha.
Food Prefers leaves and flowers; seeds and fruit to lesser extent. Readily climbs into low bushes and trees to harvest.
Reproduction 1–3 fully haired young, weighing 14.7 g average, born after gestation of about 90 days. Young born in rock crevice, usually lined with dry plant material, which might be harvested by Namaqua rock mice. Births linked to summer rains. Female has 2 pairs thoracic mammae behind shoulder-blades and protruding from sides, with 3rd pair abdominal mammae also along sides.
Longevity Not recorded, but one animal (clear identifying mark) lived in the wild for at least 3 years in Namib.
Calls Alarm squeak but no other calls recorded.
Occurrence Limited to western escarpment and adjacent areas. Etosha, Namib-Naukluft, Fish River (Namibia); Richtersveld, Goegap, Namaqua, Augrabies (South Africa).

MEASUREMENTS
Weight: 160–250 g
Total length: 30 cm
Tail length: 14 cm

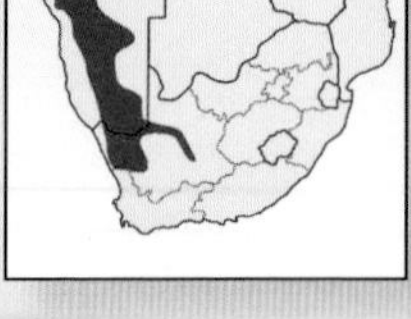

GIANT RAT

Cricetomys gambianus

Afrikaans: *Reuserot* **German:** *Riesenhamsterratte* **French:** *Rat de Gambie*

Identification pointers Largest 'rat-like' rodent in the region. Long, whip-like tail, white for slightly less than half its length towards tip. Upperparts grey to grey-brown; underparts lighter; upper sides of feet pale grey to white. Short, dark hair around eyes; ears large, thin and highly mobile.

Similar Exotic house rat (*Rattus rattus*) and brown rat (*R. norvegicus*) smaller, lack white on tail and ears not as prominent.

Habitat Forest and woodland, primarily in higher rainfall far east.

Behaviour Mainly nocturnal, but may be active during day if undisturbed. Digs own burrows but also uses holes, hollow trees and piles of plant debris. Surplus food carried in large cheek pouches to store in den. When occupied, burrow is usually closed from inside; may have as many as 3 entrances. Home range relatively small, usually 1–4 ha, and seldom exceeds 10 ha. Marks home range, but level of territoriality unknown.

Mainly terrestrial, but can climb well.

Food Fruit, seeds, grains, bulbs, tubers and leaves; gains most of its water from food, but will drink readily. Occasionally eats insects, snails and crabs.

Reproduction 2–4 (rarely 1 or 5) young, weighing 20–30 g average, born after gestation of 28–36 (average 30–32) days. Births take place in summer. Young remain in burrow for at least 40 days after birth; leave nest permanently at about 80 days. Female has 2 pairs pectoral, 2 pairs inguinal mammae.

Longevity A captive individual lived for 7 years and 10 months; other records mention 4 years.

Calls Bird-like chirrup or piping communication; hisses when alarmed.

Occurrence Restricted to far eastern parts of region, with an isolated population in the Soutpansberg and Blouberg ranges in Limpopo province. Mana Pools (Zimbabwe); Kruger, iSimangaliso, Ndumo (South Africa).

MEASUREMENTS
Weight: 1–3 kg
Total length: 80 cm
Tail length: 42 cm

Right front

24 mm
without claws

Right back
32 mm
without claws

109

POUCHED MOUSE
Saccostomus campestris

Afrikaans: *Wangsakmuis* **German:** *Kurzschwanz-Hamsterratte* **French:** *Souris à poche*

Identification pointers Round and fat-bodied, with soft, silky grey or greyish-brown fur. Underparts and lower face white. Tail length less than head-and-body length; tail pale to white in colour. Legs short. Ears short and rounded; eyes small. Variable in size and colour throughout range. Bears strong resemblance to domesticated hamster.

Similar Smaller fat mouse has brown, not greyish upperparts.

Habitat Prefers soft, particularly sandy, soils. Open and dense woodland, as well as rocky areas.

Behaviour Nocturnal and terrestrial. Generally solitary, although may live in loose colonies. Digs own burrow, but will also use burrows excavated by other species; also seeks shelter in termite mounds, under logs and rock piles. Uses pouches in cheeks to take substantial quantities of food to shelter or burrow, where it can be eaten in safety from predators or stored for future use. Quite slow moving and easy to catch by hand; otherwise quite difficult to trap.

Food Seeds, small wild fruit and occasionally insects, especially termites.

Reproduction 2–10 fully haired pups, weighing < 3 g, born after gestation of about 20 days. Litters born mainly during wet summer months; female may have several litters in a season. Female has 3 pairs pectoral, 2 pairs inguinal mammae.

Longevity A captive lived just short of its 4th year; < 3 years usual in the wild.

Calls Typical mouse-like chittering and squeaks if handled.

Occurrence Widespread in the region but absent from much of the arid west and the southeast. Fairly common and present in many protected areas. Etosha, Khaudom, Waterberg, Caprivi (Namibia); Okavango, Chobe, Central Kalahari, Nxai Pan (Botswana); Hwange, Mana Pools, Gonarezhou (Zimbabwe); Mapungubwe, Kruger, Marekele, Pilanesberg, Kgalagadi, Augrabies, Mokala, iSimangaliso, Greater Addo (South Africa).

MEASUREMENTS
Weight: 45–85g
Total length: 15–26 cm
Tail length: 5 cm

FAT MOUSE

Steatomys pratensis

Afrikaans: *Vetmuis* **German:** *Fettmaus* **French:** *Rat adipeux*

Identification pointers Small, dumpy, with tail about a third of total length. Upperparts rusty-brown to sandy-brown; white underparts and upper surfaces of feet. Tail usually darker above than below. During winter can lay down thick fat deposits under skin and around organs.

Similar Tiny fat mouse (*S. parvus*) and Krebs's fat mouse (*S. krebsii*) very similar; all vary considerably in size and coloration. Krebs's is only one of the 3 in the southwest of region. See pygmy mouse, but smaller and delicately built.

Habitat Favours areas with sandy soils; associated with cultivated fields.

Behaviour Nocturnal and terrestrial. Apparently lives singly or in pairs. Digs own burrow, but does not form true colony. Well adapted to drought as can build up fat deposits and reduce body temperature to lower metabolism and live on fat reserves. Unlike pouched mouse, does not have cheek pouches, but does carry surplus to store in burrow.

Food Primarily seeds, but small bulbs and roots dug up too; also some green plant material and insects.

Reproduction Litter of 1–9 (3–4 more usual) pups, weighing 1.5 g average. Gestation period not known. Births probably tied to rainy season. Female has 6–8 pairs mammae, from pectoral to inguinal region.

Longevity An individual lived 3 years in captivity.

Calls Typical mouse-like calls, seldom heard by humans.

Occurrence Widespread, often common and undergoes population eruptions during prime conditions. Not hunted as food by humans in the region to the same extent as in other parts of Africa. Etosha, Khaudom, Waterberg, Caprivi (Namibia); Okavango, Moremi, Chobe (Botswana); Hwange, Mana Pools, Gonarezhou (Zimbabwe); Mapungubwe, Marakele, Kruger, Ndumo, iSimangaliso, Ithala (South Africa).

MEASUREMENTS
Weight: 26 g
Total length: 8–15 cm
Tail length: 5 cm

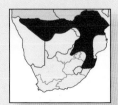

GERBIL (LARGE-EARED) MOUSE
Malacothrix typica

Afrikaans: *Bakoormuis* **German:** *Großohrmaus* **French:** *Souris à grandes oreilles*

Identification pointers Small, but easy to distinguish by short tail, very large, rounded ears and markings on back. Overall colour variable, from pale reddish-brown to buffy-grey, and variations in between, with variable dark hair 'pencilling'. Fur soft and silky. Dark patch behind each ear, dark stripe extending from just behind shoulders to rump and dark patch on top of each hip. Underparts range from greyish-white to clean white.

Similar No other species in the region has such proportionally large ears or distinctive dark patterning on upperparts.

Habitat Associated with hard soils; ground cover with short grass in north and with low Karoo bush in south. Lives in areas with annual rainfall of 150–500 mm.

Behaviour Nocturnal, terrestrial and primarily solitary. Excavates deep burrow, with entrance clean of debris; in some areas burrow near vertical, but in others more sloping. Unlike many rodents, easy to capture by hand when caught in blinding torchlight, and seldom attempts to bite. Allegedly will cover surprisingly long distances (4 km) in a night foraging.

Food Green plant material, with a small component of grass seeds; up to 10% of intake may be made up of insects, mainly termites.

Reproduction Litter of 2–8 (average 4) pups, weighing about 1 g, born after gestation of 23–27 days. Most birthing takes place during summer months (August–March). Female has 4 pairs mammae, from pectoral to inguinal region.

Longevity Approximately 2.5 years in captivity.

Calls Under stress make *dzizz-dzizz* buzzing call; also soft squeak.

Occurrence Wide range in the west and central areas of region. Etosha, Fish River (Namibia); Richtersveld, Augrabies, Kgalagadi, Namaqua, West Coast, Karoo, Willem Pretorius (South Africa).

MEASUREMENTS
Weight: 15–20 g
Total length: 11 cm
Tail length: 3.5 cm

CAPE SHORT-TAILED GERBIL
Desmodillus auricularis

Afrikaans: *Kaapse kortstertspringmuis* **German:** *Kurzschwanz-Rennmaus*
French: *Gerbille à queue courte du Cap*

Identification pointers Dumpy appearance; only gerbil in the region with tail shorter than head-and-body length. Ears narrow and rounded at tip; white patch of hair at base of each ear; underparts pure white. Coloration variable across region and within any single population; brownish-buff, cinnamon-buff, grey-brown to pale greyish-brown upperparts most common, but most variations in between.

Similar Other gerbils within its range (5 species) all have tails equal to, or slightly longer than, head-and-body length.

Habitat Prefers harder ground, with some grass or low scrub cover. In Namib Desert on gravel plains, often with minimal vegetation cover. Barely occurs within areas receiving > 500 mm annual rainfall.

Behaviour Nocturnal and terrestrial. Constructs own burrow, digging 2 types: sloping with a mound of soil at entrance, and near-vertical without soil at entrance, probably excavated from underground. In some parts of region may be social and not solitary, but in other areas burrow occupied by single individual. Same-sex conflicts occur, as well as between male and female.

Food Seeds, mostly of grasses, and some green plant material make up bulk of food. In at least part of range eats large quantities of insects, especially termites. Some food carried back to burrow.

Reproduction Litter of 1–7 (average 3) pups, weighing about 3.6 g, born after gestation of about 21 days. Breeding throughout year. Female has 2 pairs pectoral, 2 pairs inguinal mammae.

Longevity Up to 3 years in captivity.

Calls Highly modulated trill, varying in length and frequency.

Occurrence Common and abundant across much of its range. Etosha, Skeleton Coast, Namib-Naukluft, Fish River (Namibia); Nxai Pan, Makgadikgadi, Central Kalahari (Botswana); Richtersveld, Namaqua, West Coast, Augrabies, Kgalagadi, Pilanesberg, Madikwe, Willem Pretorius, Mokala, Karoo (South Africa).

MEASUREMENTS
Weight: 39–70 g (50 g)
Total length: 20 cm
Tail length: 9 cm

HAIRY-FOOTED GERBIL

Gerbillurus paeba

Afrikaans: *Haarpootspringmuis* **German:** *Zwergrennmaus* **French:** *Gerbille à pieds velus*

Identification pointers One of 4 species of 'hairy-footed' gerbils in the region; this species most widespread and abundant. Small, with tail longer than head-and-body length. Upperparts pale reddish-brown, or greyish-red, 'pencilled' with dark brown hairs. Tail same colour as upperparts. Pure white underparts, including chin and inner leg surfaces. Numerous short hairs on underside of hind feet.

Similar Brush-tailed hairy-footed gerbil has a prominent tassel at tail-tip; found in limited area of southern Namibia and adjacent Northern Cape. Dune and Setzer's hairy-footed gerbils restricted to limited areas of Namib Desert.

Habitat Desert and semi-desert areas, but extends into Mozambique and to South Africa's south coast, where inhabits dunes.

Behaviour Nocturnal and solitary. Excavates simple burrow, with single entrance and tunnel in Namib Desert, but elsewhere more complex. Burrow entrance usually hidden at base of bush. Where sand very loose may burrow where antelope have urinated, giving a solidified working base. Home range size varies under different conditions, 1–8 ha, but usually < 4 ha.

Food Omnivore, takes small invertebrates, seeds and other plant material.

Reproduction Litter of 2–5 (average 3–4) pups born after gestation of about 21 days. May breed at any time of year, but some areas have peak related to onset of rains. Female has 1 or 2 pairs pectoral, 2 pairs inguinal mammae.

Longevity > 2 years in captivity.

Calls Mouse-like squeaks when handled; produces several ultrasonic sounds, including clicks.

Occurrence Skeleton Coast, Etosha, Namib-Naukluft, Fish River, Waterberg, Khaudom (Namibia); Central Kalahari, Nxai Pan, Makgadikgadi (Botswana); Kgalagadi, Mapungubwe, Augrabies, Namaqua, Richtersveld, Agulhas, West Coast, Tankwa, Karoo, Camdeboo, Mountain Zebra, Greater Addo (South Africa).

MEASUREMENTS
Weight: 25 g
Total length: 20 cm
Tail length: 11 cm

BUSHVELD GERBIL

Gerbilliscus leocogaster

Afrikaans: *Bosveldspringmuis* **German:** *Weißbauch-Nacktsohlenrennmaus*
French: *Gerbille du bushveld*

Identification pointers Typical large 'mouse-like' gerbil. Tail longer than head-and-body length, normally has distinctive darker line along upperside, tip never white. Ears relatively long, not as narrow as in hairy-footed gerbils. *Gerbilliscus* gerbils sometimes referred to as 'naked sole' gerbils, in contrast to 'hairy-footed' group. Fur soft, reddish-brown to yellow-buff on upperparts (palest animals in west); white underparts. White patch above and behind each eye.

Similar Highveld gerbil (*Gerbilliscus brantsii*) very variable in colour, but mostly light reddish-brown to pale fawn-russet; underparts white to buff-grey; no dark line on upper tail; many have part of tail white; range overlaps extensively. Hairy-footed gerbil has much smaller, narrow ears.

Habitat Areas with sandy soil, from semi-desert to woodland savanna.

Behaviour Strictly nocturnal, sheltering during day in self-excavated burrows. Lives in loosely knit colonies. Burrow entrances usually at base of a low bush or grass clump. Although a burrow is usually occupied by a pair, it is suspected that many burrows within a colony may be interconnected.

Food Omnivorous, often taking an equal mix of plant parts, especially seeds and leaves, and insects.

Reproduction Litter of 2–9 (average 5) pups, weighing about 2.8 g, born after gestation of some 28 days. In some parts of range breeds through year, in other areas tied to summer rains. Female has 2 pairs pectoral, 2 pairs inguinal mammae.

Longevity An Asian 'naked-soled' gerbil lived for 7 years in captivity.

Calls Ultrasonic calls include whistles, *peeps*, trill; some audible.

Occurrence Widespread in savanna and semi-arid country across north of region, and as far south as South Africa's Free State. Generally very common but subject to peaks and dips.

MEASUREMENTS
Weight: 32–114 g
 (average 70 g)
Total length: 21–33 cm
 (average 28 cm)
Tail length: 12–17 cm
 (average 15 cm)

NAMAQUA ROCK MOUSE

Micaelamys namaquensis

Afrikaans: *Namakwa-klipmuis* **German:** *Namaqua Felsenmaus* **French:** *Rat des rochers du Namaqua*

Identification pointers Tail length generally greater than head-and-body length, but much variation across its great range. Coloration also variable, but upperparts usually reddish-brown to yellowish-fawn, with all variations in between; often with black pencilling. Underparts from dirty white to greyish-white. Upper surfaces of feet may be white, grey-white to fawn.

Similar Grant's rock mouse has generally greyer coat, and tail equal to head-and-body length; occurs in south of South Africa. Red veld rat similar, but averages larger; occupies range of habitats, not just rocks. 'Naked sole' gerbils only on sandy soils, never in rocks.

Habitat Largely restricted to rocky habitats, but in Kalahari also open bush and woodland country; also in southeast of range.

Behaviour Nocturnal and mainly terrestrial, but will climb readily and well. Lives in small colony in communal shelter, which characteristically has large accumulations of dry grass and other plant material dragged into the entrance. Shelters are often located in horizontal rock crevices and cracks, and occasionally in trees. Will also dig burrow at base of bush and occasionally moves into stick lodge of bush Karoo rat. In hot, dry areas will aestivate to save water and energy.

Food Seeds of grass and other plants, and green material; occasionally takes insects.

Reproduction 1–7 (usually 3–5) pups, weighing 2.5 g average. Young nipple-cling to mother for up to 21 days, and are dragged around as she forages. Seasonal birth differences across region. Female has 1 pair pectoral, 2 pairs inguinal mammae.

Longevity No records, but probably < 2 years.

Calls Typical mouse-like squeaks, also very low chitter.

Occurrence Only absent from Namib Desert and Mozambique plain. Very common to super abundant.

MEASUREMENTS
Weight: 33–58 g
(average 50 g)
Total length: 18–34 cm
(average 26 cm)
Tail length: 10–19 cm
(average 15 cm)

ACACIA RAT
BLACK-TAILED TREE RAT

Thallomys paedulcus
Thallomys nigricaudatus

Afrikaans: *Akasiarot,* Swartstertakasiarot **German:** *Akazienratte, Schwarzschwanz-Baummaus*
French: *Rat des acacias, Souris arboricole à queue noire*

Identification pointers These 2 arboreal rats cannot be separated in field, differing only in chromosomal make-up, therefore description applies to both. Tail longer than head-and-body length, brown or black in colour; in many specimens tail is paler from base, becoming darker or black over most of its length. Upperparts variable colour, but usually grey-brown (often with yellowish-brown wash) and visibly grizzled with black hairs. Much variation even within any single population. Underparts bright white. Dark ring around eye usually present, but varies in intensity. Ears large, rounded and prominent.

Similar No other similar arboreal rodent within range; seldom descends to ground.

Habitat Savanna woodland, particularly areas dominated by acacia trees, especially camelthorn (*Acacia erioloba*). Often associated with watercourses, where these trees often grow.

Behaviour Nocturnal and arboreal. Lives in tree hole, but may also make use of large bird's nest. Large amount of nesting material often sticks out of tree hole. Each nest may be occupied by a pair and their offspring, but several adults may occupy same nest. Leaves nest to forage after sunset and moves from tree to tree through canopy. Occurs in many park camps; curious and will watch humans with interest.

Food Green leaves, green twigs, fresh seeds and pods, as well as some insects. Often carries green twigs back to nest.

Reproduction 2–5 pups, weighing about 2.5 g, mainly born during summer months (August–April).

Longevity A captive lived 3 years 6 months.

Calls Twittering call when individuals meet.

Occurrence Wide range in north of region, penetrating Namib Desert along vegetated river courses in west, to high-rainfall coastal plain of Mozambique in east.

MEASUREMENTS
Weight: 64–110 g
  (average 100 g)
Total length: 24–35 cm
  (average 30 cm)
Tail length: 17 cm

THICKET RATS

Grammomys spp.

Afrikaans: *Woudmuise* **German:** *Waldmäuse* **French:** *Souris des bois*

Identification pointers Three species of thicket rat in the region: woodland, Mozambique woodland and Macmillan's; all very similar in appearance and difficult to separate in field. Slender, very long tail diagnostic. Upperparts vary in colour from reddish-brown with greyish tinge to much more grey-brown; underparts bright white. Ears large and prominent. Mozambique species sometimes has white patch at base of ear.

Similar Black-tailed tree and acacia rats much larger and partially black tailed; share arboreal habit.

Habitat Forest and dense woodland; although most widespread woodland thicket rat also found in more open woodland types, as well as in extensive reed beds.

Behaviour Nocturnal and arboreal. Construct nests of grass and other fine plant material in vegetation tangles up to 2 m from ground. Will also make use of tree holes and even weaver-bird nests.

It has been reported that several adults and litters of pups may share the same nest; nests seen by the authors contained only one female and young. One female constructed a nest in a rucksack, where she deposited her litter of 4 pups.

Food Seasonal and regional differences, but take seeds, wild fruit, green material and bark.

Reproduction 2–5 (rarely 7) pups, weighing about 4 g, born after gestation of about 24 days. Pups nipple-cling for up to 26 days. Probably breeds throughout year, but with summer peak in some areas.

Longevity A captive woodland thicket rat lived > 4 years 5 months.

Calls None known.

Occurrence Mainly restricted to eastern coastal plain. Kruger, iSimangaliso, Ndumo, Thembe, uMkhuze, Greater Addo (South Africa).

MEASUREMENTS
Weight: 24–52 g
  (average 30 g)
Total length: 20–30 cm
  (average 27 cm)
Tail length: 14–20 cm
  (average 17 cm)

FOUR-STRIPED GRASS MOUSE

Rhabdomys pumilio

Afrikaans: *Streepmuis* **German:** *Vierstreifengrasmaus* **French:** *Rat à quatre raies*

Identification pointers Four distinct longitudinal stripes running down back. Colour variable from dark russet-brown to almost grey-white upperparts. Underparts vary from off-white to pale grey-brown. Darker animals tend to be found in higher-rainfall areas, paler animals in drier regions. Backs of ears, and often snout, russet to yellowish-brown.

Similar Single-striped grass mouse, but has one black stripe down centre of back.

Habitat Desert fringe to high-rainfall montane areas. Grass must be present. Sea level to 2 700 m.

Behaviour Diurnal, although sometimes active at night, especially during summer months. Digs burrow system, with well-hidden entrance, from which foraging runways radiate. In some areas occupies stick-lodge of bush Karoo rat (*Otomys unisulcatus*), and quite commonly commensal with man. Will construct domed nest in dense grass clumps and termite mounds. Some evidence that female becomes territorial and defensive when she has a litter.

Food Seeds as well as other plant parts; insects also taken. Seasonal variations in diet.

Reproduction Litter of 2–9 (usually 5–6) pups, weighing 2.5 g average, born after gestation of about 23–25 days. Between 2 and 5 litters per season is usual. Females may be pregnant any time of year, but most birthing during summer months (September–April). Female has 2 pairs pectoral, 2 pairs inguinal mammae.

Longevity A captive lived 2 years 11 months; averages 1.5 months in the wild, but up to 2 years.

Calls Typical mouse-like squeaks and twitters.

Occurrence Very widespread and common, but absent from large parts of north-central Botswana, southern and northern Zimbabwe and Mozambique; occurs virtually throughout South Africa and much of Namibia. In all conservation areas within its range.

MEASUREMENTS
Weight: 30–85 g
 (average 40 g)
Total length: 18–21 cm
Tail length: 8–11 cm

Right front

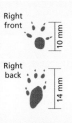

10 mm

Right back

14 mm

119

PYGMY MOUSE

Mus minutoides

Afrikaans: *Dwergmuis* **German:** *Afrikanische Zwergmaus* **French:** *Souris pygmée d'Afrique*

Identification pointers Most common of the 6 species of pygmy mice. Very small, delicate, with tail shorter than head-and-body length. Fairly prominent, rounded ears, sometimes small, white patch at ear base. Upperparts range from light fawn to dark russet-brown, with some black hair 'pencilling'. Underparts and upper foot surfaces white.

Similar Five species of pygmy mice difficult to separate. Setzer's and grey-bellied have very limited ranges in far north. Desert pygmy does not overlap; found in eastern Namibia and across Botswana, Neave's pygmy overlaps with pygmy mouse in northeast.

Habitat Fynbos to savanna grassland and woodland; arid areas to high-rainfall zones; sea level to about 2 400 m.

Behaviour Nocturnal and terrestrial. Solitary, in pairs or female and young, but not communal. Digs own burrow in soft soils, but also uses burrow dug by other species, or shelters under vegetation debris,

rocks. Commonly associates with larger rodent species, making use of their runways.

Food Seeds (especially those of grass) and green plant material, but also some insects. Seasonal and regional variations.

Reproduction Litter of 1–7 (usually 4) pups, weighing < 1 g, born after gestation of 19 days. Probably breeds year-round, with seasonal peaks. Male stays with female and litter in nest after birth; both defend against intruders. Female has 2 pairs pectoral, 1 pair abdominal, 2 pairs inguinal mammae.

Longevity A captive reportedly lived for just over 3 years; probably much less in the wild.

Calls Quiet twittering.

Occurrence Present across south and east of region. Augrabies, West Coast, Namaqua, Tankwa, Agulhas, Karoo, Mokala, Garden Route, Greater Addo, Camdeboo, Mountain Zebra, Willem Pretorius, Golden Gate, Kruger, Mapungubwe, iSimangaliso, uKhahlamba, Ithala, Ndumo, uMkhuze (South Africa).

MEASUREMENTS
Weight: 2–12 g
(average 6 g)
Total length: 8–11 cm
(average 10 cm)
Tail length: 4–6 cm

CAPE SPINY MOUSE

Acomys subspinosus

Afrikaans: *Kaapse stekelmuis* **German:** *Kap-Stachelmaus* **French:** *Souris épineuse du Cap*

Identification pointers Mouse-like appearance. Recognizable by sharp, spiny hair growing on back. Tail slightly shorter than head-and-body length; as it breaks easily, a fair number have shortened tails. Upperparts dark grey to russet-grey-brown with dark 'pencilling', giving grizzled appearance. Underparts and upper surfaces of feet white.

Similar Spiny mouse (*A. spinosissimus*), but widely separated distributions; no other species within range has spine-like hairs on back. Pygmy rock mouse has no spines; shares crevices in limited area.

Habitat Rocky areas on mountain slopes, hills and flat-rock escarpments; all within fynbos vegetation system. Sea level to about 1 200 m.

Behaviour Nocturnal and terrestrial. Single or in small groups; possibly family parties or related animals. Shelters in rock crevices and cracks, but in some areas shelters in burrows. On western escarpment uses only cracks and crevices, shared with Barbour's pygmy rock mouse, Namaqua rock mouse, spectacled dormouse and Cape rock sengi. Adapts well to captivity, becomes quite tame.

Food Grass and other seeds, as well as some green plant material. Takes fairly high numbers of invertebrates, including termites, small beetles, millipedes and snails.

Reproduction 3 pups, weighing 3.3 g average, born after gestation of > 32 days. Young well developed for such a small rodent. In some species other females help clean newborns and sever umbilical cord. Female has 2–3 pairs mammae.

Longevity Other *Acomys* spp. have lived 3–5 years in captivity.

Calls Squeaks, though seldom heard; sometimes barely audible buzzing sound.

Occurrence Restricted almost entirely to South Africa's Western Cape. Cedarberg, West Coast, Table Mountain, Agulhas, Bontebok, Garden Route (South Africa). Spiny mouse found in most Zimbabwean conservation areas; Kruger, Mapungubwe, Marakele (South Africa).

MEASUREMENTS
Weight: 13–26 g
(average 22 g)
Total length: 14–19 cm
(average 17 cm)
Tail length: 6.5–10 cm
(average 8 cm)

BUSH KAROO RAT

Otomys unisulcatus

Afrikaans: *Boskaroorot* **German:** *Karoo-Lamellenzahnratte* **French:** *Rat du Karoo*

Identification pointers Stocky, with relatively short tail. Ears as long as broad, with rounded tips. Blunt-snouted; overall appearance a bit like guineapig with a tail. Colour variable across range, but usually shades of grey-brown, 'pencilled' with black hairs, giving overall grizzled appearance. Underside of tail lighter than top. May have reddish infusion around snout, eyes and sometimes ears.

Similar Other members of genus *Otomys* do not occur in same habitats. Shares large part of its range with 2 whistling rats (*Parotomys* spp.); similar but they live in burrows, without stick lodges, and have distinctive whistling call.

Habitat Arid to semi-arid areas; favours light to moderate ground cover of low karroid bush and scattered open thicket country. Often in broken, rocky terrain but not mountain country.

Behaviour Strictly diurnal. Only rodent that constructs large lodges (up to 2.3 m diameter, 70 cm height) with sticks, sometimes adding bones, sheep wool and animal droppings. On west coast often adds 'tiling' of mussel shells to outer dome. Lodges occupied by 1–11 rats; usually at base of bush (often thorny) or among rocks. Pathways link lodges and lead to feeding grounds. Lodges have outer 'platforms' for defecating, sunning and feeding.

Food Green plant matter, a few flowers and wild fruit.

Reproduction Litter of 2–5 (usually 2–3) pups, weighing 10–14 g, born after gestation of about 38 days. Births recorded throughout year. Female has 2 pairs inguinal mammae.

Longevity Not known for this species, but other *Otomys* spp. < 2 years.

Calls When alarmed, rapidly flicks tail, making swishing sound; squabbling squeaks.

Occurrence Restricted to the south of the region, entirely within South Africa. Namaqua, West Coast, Karoo, Mountain Zebra, Greater Addo.

MEASUREMENTS
Weight: 78–176 g
(average 125 g)
Total length: 17–29 cm
(average 24 cm)
Tail length: 7–11 cm
(average 9 cm)

WOODLAND DORMOUSE

Graphiurus murinus

Afrikaans: *Boswaaierstertmuis* **German:** *Afrikanischer Waldbilch* **French:** *Graphiure des bois*

Identification pointers Squirrel-like rodent, with bushy tail and prominent, rounded ears. Upperparts uniform grey to grey with brown-fawnish tinge; tail grey, but often with slightly darker brown infusion above. Underparts buffy-white to pale grey-white, often a rusty tinge to at least chest. Upper surface of hands and feet white. Cheek patches and lips white or greyish-white.
Similar Smaller than any squirrels. Larger spectacled dormouse has distinctive black-and-white facial markings and more white in tail. Rock dormouse has less distinct facial pattern than spectacled, and usually has white-tipped tail. Lesser savanna dormouse cannot be separated from woodland in field; occurs in north of region. Spectacled and rock are rock crevice dwellers.
Habitat Woodland savanna and bush thicket, also in association with man-made structures. Occurs from sea level to about 2 700 m.
Behaviour Nocturnal and arboreal, will occasionally forage on ground. Several may share same nest, but foraging is solitary. Builds substantial nest of grass, leaves and lichen, in tree holes, as well as in buildings; takes over bird nestboxes and weaver-bird nests. Appears to go into full hibernation for at least part of winter.
Food Seeds and insects, with seasonal and regional differences. Also takes geckos, fledglings and possibly small, roosting birds.
Reproduction Litter of 2–4 pups, weighing about 3.5 g, born after gestation of about 24 days. Most births during summer months, but also some at other times. Female has 4 pairs mammae.
Longevity A captive lived 5 years 9 months.
Calls Twitters; loud shriek when handled, or conflict between individuals.
Occurrence Etosha, Waterberg, Khaudom, Caprivi (Namibia); Okavango, Moremi, Chobe, Central Kalahari (Botswana); Mana Pools, Hwange, Gonarezhou (Zimbabwe); all in east of South Africa, also Greater Addo, Garden Route and Agulhas in the south.

MEASUREMENTS
Weight: 30 g
Total length: 16 cm
Tail length: 7 cm

SPECTACLED DORMOUSE

Graphiurus ocularis

Afrikaans: *Gemsbokmuis* **German:** *Brillenbilch* **French:** *Graphiure à lunettes*

Identification pointers Largest of region's 4 dormice, with characteristic bushy tail and unique black-and-white facial pattern. Facial pattern includes dark ring around each eye, the 'spectacles', dark line running from sides of muzzle onto shoulders. Upperparts grey with silvery-grizzled appearance; underparts lighter, with white on cheeks, throat, underparts (sometimes grey) and upper surfaces of feet. Tail usually rimmed and white tipped.
Similar Other dormice much smaller and lack clear facial markings. Range only overlaps marginally with one other species, woodland dormouse in extreme southeast. Apart from Southern African ground squirrel, no other squirrels occur within its range, and all are much larger.
Habitat Associated with rocky and mountainous areas, also climbs trees and enters human structures. Low- and higher-rainfall areas.
Behaviour Nocturnal, mainly terrestrial, but does climb trees and bushes, and particularly agile even on sheer rock faces. Home range in one area from 1– 3.8 ha, with evidence that male and female maintain territories, in pairs or as individuals. In captivity strange animals are aggressive towards one another and will fight viciously. Not clear whether they hibernate, but will apparently go into torpor for about a month if food is in short supply.
Food Insects, millipedes, spiders, snails, scorpions; vertebrates taken include small birds, lizards and occasional frogs.
Reproduction 4–6 young born every 6–8 weeks under optimal conditions; otherwise every 6 months recorded. Births recorded in spring and summer.
Longevity A captive lived 6 years; at least 4 years in the wild.
Calls Powerful growl when threatened or during interaction between individuals.
Occurrence Fairly common. Cedarberg, Namaqua, Karoo, Camdeboo, Mountain Zebra, Greater Addo (South Africa).

MEASUREMENTS
Weight: 80 g
Total length: 22–25 cm
Tail length: 10 cm

TREE SQUIRREL

Paraxerus cepapi

Afrikaans: *Boomeekhoring* **German:** *Buschhörnchen* **French:** *Écureuil des bois*

Identification pointers Small, typical squirrel-like appearance, bushy tail and no markings. Coat grizzled sandy or greyish or yellow-brown, with lighter to white-coloured underparts, flanks often 'brighter' yellowish-brown. Animals in west of region mostly grey; those in east predominantly brown. Melanistic, or black, animals and groups known from area of Lake Mutirikwe, Zimbabwe.

Similar Striped tree squirrel (*Funisciurus congicus*) in northwest Namibia is small, with white stripe running down each side. Sun squirrel (*Heliosciurus mutabilis*) in extreme northeast (Mozambique) is larger, with series of narrow, whitish bands on tail. Red bush squirrel (*Paraxerus palliatus*) is grizzled dark grey to black, underparts and tail reddish or yellowish.

Habitat Savanna woodland types, but not true forest.

Behaviour Diurnal and will forage in trees and on ground. Seen singly or in mother and young groups, but several animals live in loose association. Adult male, or males, in a group will defend a territory against outside squirrels. Groups establish territories that average 2–4 ha, marked by mouth-wiping, urination and secretions from anal glands. Clear hierarchy in each group, with dominant adult male. Spends a lot of time basking.

Food Plant food, including leaves, fruit, flowers, seeds and tree bark, also insects.

Reproduction 1–3 (average 2) pups, weighing some 10 g, born after gestation of about 55 days. Young born in a leaf-lined tree hole. Most litters in summer, but can be expected any time of year. Females have 1 pair pectoral, 1 pair abdominal and 1 pair inguinal mammae.

Longevity Similar-sized *Funisciurus* squirrels have lived 5–9 years in captivity.

Calls Harsh chattering scold, usually accompanied by tail flicking; bird-like *chek-chik-chik*; high-pitched whistle; very vocal.

Occurrence Virtually all conservation areas across savanna zone.

MEASUREMENTS
Weight: 100–260 g
Total length: 29–36 cm
Tail length: 15–18 cm

Right
front

25 mm without claws

Right
back

46 mm without claws

125

SOUTHERN AFRICAN GROUND SQUIRREL

Xerus inauris

Afrikaans: *Grondeekhoring* **German:** *Südafrikanisches Erdhörnchen* **French:** *Écureuil foisseur*

Identification pointers Entirely terrestrial and fossorial, yet typically squirrel-like. Very small ears and fairly large, white-ringed eyes. Upperparts usually cinnamon-brown; some animals more grey-brown, with overall grizzled appearance. Single white stripe along each side of body from shoulder to thigh. Underparts greyish to white-tinged, with light brown in mid-belly. Long, bushy tail is grizzled black and white. White incisors.

Similar Damara ground squirrel (*X. princeps*) along Namib Desert fringe, where both occur; only real difference, this one has orange-coloured incisors and is largely solitary.

Habitat Open, arid areas with sparse cover and a hard substrate, also sandy areas.

Behaviour Diurnal, terrestrial and fossorial. Gregarious, living in groups of 5–30 animals. Excavates extensive burrow systems. Females and young remain in close proximity to burrows, but males live in separate burrow systems, moving from colony to colony. Frequently stands on hind legs to enhance view. Bushy tail often held over body and head when feeding, to form a 'sunshade'. Burrow systems often shared with suricate and yellow mongoose.

Food Grass, roots, seeds and bulbs; insects, particularly termites.

Reproduction 1–3 naked, helpless pups, weighing some 20 g, born after gestation of about 45 days. First leave burrow around 6 weeks old. Litters born any time of year, and females may have up to 3 litters in a year. Female has 2 pairs inguinal mammae.

Longevity A captive lived 6 years; probably 3–5 years in the wild.

Calls High-pitched whistle-alarm call, especially when birds of prey sighted; growls and 'chunters' in interactions; younger animals have a *tschip-tschip* call.

Occurrence Etosha, Namib-Naukluft, Fish River (Namibia); Central Kalahari, Nxai Pan, Makgadikgadi (Botswana); Augrabies, Kgalagadi, Pilanesberg, Camdeboo (South Africa).

MEASUREMENTS
Weight: 500 g–1 kg
(average 650 g)
Total length: 40–50 cm
Tail length: 19–25 cm

Right front
41 mm without claws

Right back
60 mm without claws

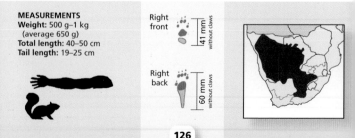

SCRUB HARE

Lepus saxatilis

Afrikaans: *Kolhaas* **German:** *Buschhase* **French:** *Lièvre des buissons*

Identification pointers Typical hare-like appearance; very long ears, short, fluffy black-and-white tail; hind legs well developed, and much longer than forelegs. Upperparts strongly black grizzled brown-grey to grey; underparts bright white; sides of face and around eyes lighter (whitish to buff) coloured; hair on nape reddish-brown. Often a spot of white hair on forehead. Animals largest in southwest, becoming smaller to north and east. In east and northeast sometimes different species recognized, savanna hare (*L. victoriae*), but impossible to separate the two.

Similar Cape hare over much of range; smaller, often has reddish-brown hair on flanks, lacks white forehead spot; found in more open country. Red rock rabbits (*Pronolagus* spp.) have shorter ears, reddish-brown tail, in rocky habitat.

Habitat Woodland and areas with scrub and grass. Common in cultivated areas.

Behaviour Nocturnal and crepuscular, but may be active on cooler, overcast days.

Spends day lying up in a form. May occur at high densities, but solitary animals, except when female is in oestrus and may be accompanied by males. Relies on camouflage when approached, running away at last minute. Stays under cover during rain and on very cold nights.

Food Grasses, but also eats leaves of some forbs and herbaceous plants.

Reproduction 1–3 well-developed leverets, weighing 115 g average, born after gestation of about 42 days. Litters may be produced any time of year, but birth peak occurs during summer months. Female has 3 pairs abdominal/inguinal mammae.

Longevity Related hare species live 7–12 years in captivity; probably less in the wild.

Calls Loud chirps, probably communication between individuals; gnashes teeth; emits loud screams when handled, or caught by predator.

Occurrence Common and widespread throughout region, but absent from Namib Desert. In virtually all conservation areas.

MEASUREMENTS
Weight: 1.5–4.5 kg
(♂ slightly larger than ♀)
Total length: 45–65 cm
Tail length: 7–17 cm

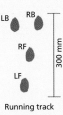

Running track

CAPE HARE

Lepus capensis

Afrikaans: *Vlakhaas* **German:** *Kaphase* **French:** *Lièvre du Cap*

Identification pointers Typical hare-like appearance; long ears; hind legs much longer than forelegs; short, fluffy tail black above and white below. Over much of range upperparts grizzled greyish-brown, with white abdomen and brownish-pink nape patch; flanks often orange-buff. In Namib Desert animals pale grey with wholly white underparts. No white spot on forehead.

Similar Scrub hare; larger, lacks orange-buff hairs on flanks, occupies less open habitat. Red rock rabbits have shorter ears, shorter back legs, reddish-brown tail, occupy rocky habitats.

Habitat Drier, open areas, especially short grassland; avoids dense scrub and woodland.

Behaviour Nocturnal and crepuscular, but will feed on cooler, overcast days. Lies up in form, but in Namib Desert will also excavate shallow burrow. When threatened, will remain still until closely approached, then run off at speed following a zigzag course. Solitary, except when female in

oestrus and accompanied by several males.

Food Grass and browse from forbs and low bushes. Latter important during dry season.

Reproduction 1–3 (average 2) leverets, weighing about 85 g, born after gestation of some 42 days. Female may have several litters in a year. Young may be born any time of year, but distinct birthing peak in summer. Female has 3 pairs abdominal/inguinal mammae.

Longevity Eurasian hare has lived > 7 years in captivity; probably 3–5 years in the wild.

Calls Gnashes teeth, but seldom heard; harsh scream if hurt or handled.

Occurrence Largely restricted to west and centre of region, with apparently isolated populations in east-central Botswana, as well as northern South Africa and adjacent area of Mozambique. Etosha, Skeleton Coast, Namib-Naukluft, Fish River (Namibia); Richtersveld, Namaqua, West Coast, Augrabies, Kgalagadi, Pilanesberg, Willem Pretorius, Camdeboo (South Africa).

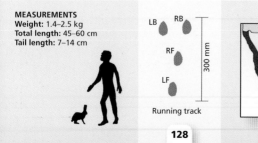

MEASUREMENTS
Weight: 1.4–2.5 kg
Total length: 45–60 cm
Tail length: 7–14 cm

LB RB

RF

300 mm

LF

Running track

SMITH'S RED ROCK RABBIT

Pronolagus rupestris

Afrikaans: *Smith-rooiklipkonyn* **German:** *Smith-Rotkaninchen* **French:** *Lapin roux des rochers de Smith*

Identification pointers Rabbit-like appearance; long ears; hind legs longer than forelegs; soft, dense fur. Grizzled grey-brown upperparts and reddish-brown on flanks, limbs and tail, with lighter (not white) underparts. Ears grey to grey-brown; usually patch of reddish fur on nape between ears.

Similar Two hare species have longer ears and hind legs, black-and-white tail; different habitat requirements. 3 other red rock rabbit species in the region, all very similar, but Jameson's (*P. randensis*) range does not overlap; Natal (*P. crassicaudatus*) marginally overlaps in vicinity of Drakensberg; Hewitt's (*P. saundersiae*) occurs in southern part of South Africa, overlaps with Smith's.

Habitat Rocky areas on hill slopes and mountainsides, including isolated rock outcrops with good grass and scrub cover.

Behaviour Nocturnal, but will bask and forage on overcast days. During day lies up in a form created by weight of body, or in rock crevices and among boulder clusters. Solitary forager, but in suitable habitat several animals may live in close proximity. Lozenge-shaped droppings deposited in middens that may cover several square metres.

Food Grass, but leaves of shrubs important in more arid areas.

Reproduction 1–2 pups (near-naked compared to newborn hares), weighing 40–50 g, born after gestation of about 38 days. Female makes nest of grass and sticks, lined with her belly fur. Most litters recorded September–February. Female has 3 pairs inguinal/abdominal mammae.

Longevity No records.

Calls Loud screams when alarmed, handled or trapped; may also scream with certain social interactions.

Occurrence South of region, mainly within South Africa, but also in southern Namibia and Lesotho. Augrabies, Namaqua, Agulhas, Bontebok, De Hoop, Garden Route, Karoo, Greater Addo, Mountain Zebra, Camdeboo, Willem Pretorius, Golden Gate, uKhahlamba (South Africa).

MEASUREMENTS
Weight: 1.3–2 kg
Total length: 43–65 cm
Tail length: 5–11 cm

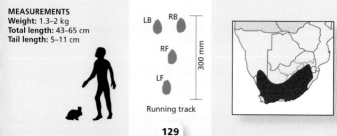

LB RB
RF
300 mm
LF

Running track

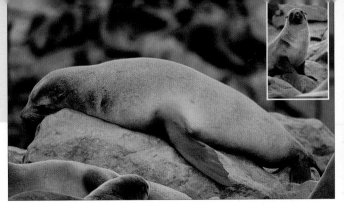

CAPE FUR SEAL

Arctocephalus pusillus

Afrikaans: *Kaapse pelsrob* **German:** *Südafrikanischer Seebär* **French:** *Otarie à fourrure d'Afrique du Sud*

Identification pointers Dark brown to golden-brown, but appears black when wet. Coarse outer hair of bull may be greyish-black with a tinge of brown; female more brownish-grey. Male much larger than female, weighing up to 360 kg in summer. Newborn pup has velvety black coat. When moving on land, hindlimbs brought forward to support some of body mass, forelimbs bend out and slightly backwards.

Similar No other seal regularly in region.

Habitat Marine, coastal and offshore islands.

Behaviour Mid-October mature bulls move to breeding sites, or rookeries, to establish territories, which are actively defended against rival bulls. Cows arrive several weeks later to give birth. A 'beach master' establishes a harem of several cows; mating takes place about 5–6 days after cow has given birth. Territories and harems break up before end of December. Remain inshore when hunting, but may go as far as edge of continental shelf.

Food Shoaling fish such as pilchards; other fish, squid and crustaceans.

Reproduction Single pup, weighing 4.5–6.5 kg, born after gestation of about 360 days. Birth late November to early December. There are 25 breeding locations, most on offshore islands, but one of the largest is on mainland at Cape Cross, Namibia. Female has 2 pairs inguinal teats (mammae form a sheet under blubber layer).

Longevity Bulls live > 20 years.

Calls Extremely vocal at rookeries; barks, growls, snarls, pig-like *oink*, among others.

Occurrence At least 1.5 million fur seals in South African and Namibian waters. Along Namibian coast, northwards into Angola; in South Africa from Namibian border on Atlantic Ocean, to about East London on Indian Ocean. Most easterly breeding rookery in Algoa Bay (Port Elizabeth). Skeleton Coast, Namib-Naukluft (Namibia); Namaqua, West Coast, Table Mountain, Agulhas, Garden Route, Greater Addo (South Africa).

MEASUREMENTS
Weight: ♂ 247–360 kg
  (average 190 kg)
  ♀ 57–120 kg (average 75 kg)
Total length: ♂ up to 2.2 m
  ♀ 1.5–1.8 m

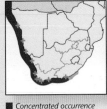

■ Concentrated occurrence
  Overall range
■ Breeding colonies

SOUTHERN RIGHT WHALE

Eubalaena australis

Afrikaans: *Suidkaper* **German:** *Südkaper* **French:** *Balaine franche australe*

Identification pointers Body dark grey-black with occasional white patches on underparts. Head very large, with deeply arched jaw-line; head and back more or less on same level. No dorsal fin, grooves or pleats on throat. Flukes are large and pointed at tips. Flippers broad-tipped. Numerous white callosities (growths) on head; largest on front of snout. 'V'-shaped blow when much of back exposed; when diving, flukes come clear of water. Only large whale seen regularly close inshore May–December.

Similar Humpback whale (*Megaptera novaeangliae*) has long, mainly white flippers, small fin well down back; often shows flippers and frequently breaches (jumps from water). Bryde's has 3 ridges on top of head; flukes and flippers do not show when dives from surface.

Habitat Coastal waters mainly on South Africa's south and southwest coasts, often very close inshore; oceanic.

Behaviour Pod consists of fewer than 12 (usually 2–3) individuals and is normally a family unit. Increasing population frequently seen in sheltered bays from Lambert's Bay to Algoa Bay. Moves into region's waters from about May to December, although many leave in October. Glides and rolls on surface, when flippers and flukes visible.

Food Plankton. Only St Helena population apparently feeds during summer; rest do not feed in region.

Reproduction Single calf, 6 m long, weighing around a ton, born after gestation of 360–390 days. Births between May and August. Female has 2 mammary slits, one each side of genital opening.

Longevity Possibly > 70 years.

Calls Quite vocal; hissing noise when spume expelled from blowhole.

Occurrence Some of best viewing sites are Table Mountain (False Bay), Hermanus (Walker Bay), De Hoop Nature Reserve, Mossel Bay, Plettenberg Bay, Algoa Bay (Port Elizabeth; Greater Addo), south coast, St Helena Bay, Lambert's Bay, West Coast (South Africa).

MEASUREMENTS
Weight: 20–30 tons
  (exceptionally 60 tons)
Total length: 14–18 m

■ Concentrated occurrence
■ Overall range

HUMPBACK DOLPHIN

Sousa chinensis

Afrikaans: *Boggelrugdolfyn* **German:** *Indopazifischer Buckeldelfin* **French:** *Dauphin à bosse du Pacifique*

Identification pointers Distinguished from other long-beaked dolphins by long, thickened ridge, or hump, along middle of back, supporting small, pointed dorsal fin. In the region most animals coloured dark-grey to brown-black; underparts off-white to grey, rarely with pinkish tinge. Slow swimmers and will spy-hop. Snout usually first part of animal to break surface.

Similar Bottlenosed dolphin, but it lacks the distinctive hump.

Habitat Inshore waters, rarely to more than 25 m depth, and will enter lagoons and estuaries, as well as feeding over shallow sand- and mud-banks.

Behaviour Groups may range from 1–30 individuals (usually 3–7), with much movement in and out of groups. Forages close inshore, favouring shallow water. Rarely ventures more than a few hundred metres from shore. Dives usually last < 1 minute, but up to 5 minutes on record. May be some seasonal movements in South African waters; most animals appear to be resident.

Food Small fish, squid, octopus and crustaceans.

Reproduction Single calf, 1 m long, weighing around 14 kg, born after gestation of 300–360 days. Young usually weaned at the age of 2 years. Cow gives birth any time of year, but with a possible peak. Female has 2 mammary slits, one each side of genital opening.

Longevity > 40 years recorded.

Calls Few audible on surface except for popping and belching sounds.

Occurrence Coastal areas of Indian Ocean in the region; unlikely to be seen west of Gouritz River estuary. One of largest populations in Algoa Bay (about 450 animals) – Greater Addo; some of best viewing in Plettenberg Bay. Quite vulnerable to disturbance, such as by boats, but in South Africa this is quite strictly controlled. Occurs along most of Mozambique coast.

MEASUREMENTS
Weight: 250–285 kg
(average 280 kg)
Total length: 1.8–3 m

■ *Concentrated occurrence*

INDO-PACIFIC BOTTLENOSED DOLPHIN *Tursiops aduncus*

Afrikaans: *Indo-Pasifiese stompneusdolfyn* **German:** *Indopazifischer Großer Tümmler*
French: *Grand dauphin de l'océan Indien*

Identification pointers Large, robust, with tall, curved dorsal fin and medium-length beak that is wide and rounded at tip. Upperparts usually uniform dark grey; paler grey sides and underparts. Usually thin, pale line running from eye to flipper, but often indistinct. Most commonly seen inshore dolphin along Indian Ocean coastline.
Similar Atlantic Ocean bottlenosed dolphin is common inshore dolphin along South African and Namibian coastline; virtually identical to Indo-Pacific; deep-water population of Atlantic bottlenosed dolphin is found in Indian Ocean, but rarely inshore. Humpback dolphin distinguished by hump on back, topped by small dorsal fin, and long beak. Other dolphins all have distinguishing markings.
Habitat Coastal and inshore waters often < 20 m deep; will enter estuaries and lagoons.
Behaviour Typical pod size 5–15 (sometimes 20–50), but sometimes hundreds and up to 1 000 may gather.

Groups of 100–200 commonly seen in Algoa Bay. Commonly mixes with other dolphin species. Have been observed in co-operative hunting, where a pod drives shoals of fish to surface, and even on to shore, or onto a sandbank.
Food Mostly fish and squid, taken mainly from sea floor, or shoals herded in co-operative action.
Reproduction Single calf, 1 m long, weighing about 14 kg, born after gestation of about 360 days. Births throughout year in the region, with peaks November–February. Female has 2 mammary slits, one each side of genital opening.
Longevity 43 years recorded.
Calls Very vocal, but rarely heard on surface.
Occurrence Common along entire Indian Ocean shoreline in the region and can be seen virtually anywhere, especially in more sheltered bays. Table Mountain (False Bay), Agulhas, Garden Route, Greater Addo, iSimangaliso (South Africa).

MEASUREMENTS
Weight: 120–230 kg
 (average 190 kg)
Total length: 2.4 m
 (maximum 2.6 m)

■ Concentrated occurrence
? Distribution unverified

DUSKY DOLPHIN

Lagenorhynchus obscurus

Afrikaans: *Donkergestreepte dolfyn* **German:** *Schwarzdelfin* **French:** *Dauphin obscur*

Identification pointers Very short, black beak. Upperparts dark grey to black, as are usually flippers and flukes; dorsal fin has light grey to white margin to trailing edge. Underparts white, separated from upperparts by broad band of light grey along flanks. Two backward-pointing blazes of blackish colour intrude into grey flanks, extending downwards from upperparts.

Similar Bottlenosed dolphin has longer beak and uniform coloration. Long-beaked common dolphin (*Delphinus capensis*) has diagnostic 'hourglass' pattern on sides, and long beak. Short-beaked Haviside's dolphin (*Cephalorhynchus heavisidii*) all along west coast of region and very close inshore; very small and stocky, dorsal fin broad-based and triangular, overall dark except for white line between flippers and tail.

Habitat Inshore from shoreline to about 50 m depth, also deeper waters.

Behaviour Typical school consists of 2–20 animals, but may be encountered in hundreds. Largest pods off west coast reach about 800 individuals, with 35 average. Group size appears to fluctuate little. Separate nursery schools of cow/calf pairs occur close inshore in summer months. When hunting, will dive to depths of 150 m. Commonly rides in bow waves of boats and ships.

Food Wide variety of fish and cephalopods, mainly squid.

Reproduction Single calf, 55–91 cm long, weighing 3–10 kg, born after gestation of 330–390 days. Possibly seasonal, as newborns mainly wash ashore in January or February. Female has 2 mammary slits, one each side of genital opening.

Longevity Records up to 36 years.

Calls Vocal, but not heard.

Occurrence West coast of South Africa, and entire coast of Namibia, extending into Angola. Generally common to very common but numbers unknown. Table Mountain, West Coast, Namaqua (South Africa); Namib-Naukluft, Skeleton Coast (Namibia).

MEASUREMENTS
Weight: 49–90 kg
  (maximum 115 kg)
Total length: 1.5–2.2 m
  (average 2.1 m)

■ *Concentrated occurrence*

DUNG IDENTIFICATION

Droppings, and sometimes the way they are deposited, may indicate the presence of a particular animal in the area. Included here is a selection of those droppings that you are most likely to encounter.

Note that the match used for comparison in some photographs is 43 mm in length. Unless stated otherwise, measurements apply to length of dung. Measurements given are averages.

ELEPHANT: Variable size; often 200 mm. Barrel-shaped. Deposited at random.

SQUARE-LIPPED RHINO: 150 mm. Barrel-shaped. Bulls deposit dung in middens, often along roadsides.

HOOK-LIPPED RHINO: 100 mm. Barrel-shaped. Middens often show clear scuffing left by hind feet.

HIPPOPOTAMUS: 100 mm. Barrel-shaped. Scattered across range. Males flick dung onto bushes/grass with tail.

PLAINS ZEBRA: 50 mm. Kidney-shaped, often with 'crack'. Scattered heaps.

WARTHOG: 50 mm. Kidney-shaped. Scattered in small heaps.

BUSHPIG: Up to 80 mm. Variable in size and form. Oblong pellets. Usually scattered.

BUFFALO: Variable size. Similar to domestic cow (cow pats). Scattered.

GIRAFFE: 30 mm. Due to height of fall, heaps usually more scattered than those of eland or greater kudu.

GREATER KUDU: 20 mm. Scattered heaps. Often concentrated in shade.

BLUE WILDEBEEST: 20 mm. Scattered heaps. Territorial bulls leave large accumulations.

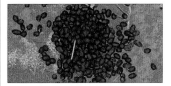

BLACK WILDEBEEST: 16 mm. Scattered heaps. Territorial bulls leave large accumulations.

RED HARTEBEEST: 17 mm. Scattered heaps. Territorial bulls leave large accumulations.

BLESBOK: 15 mm. Scattered heaps. Territorial rams may have several concentrated heaps.

ORYX/GEMSBOK: 18 mm. Scattered heaps. Concentrated bull middens; bull squats on defecating.

SABLE ANTELOPE: 18 mm. Heaps scattered at random.

IMPALA: 12–14 mm. Scattered heaps and breeding ram middens.

SPRINGBOK: 13 mm. Scattered heaps and territorial ram middens.

BUSHBUCK: 14 mm. Scattered heaps.

KLIPSPRINGER: 10 mm. Always in communal middens.

KLIPSPRINGER: Communal middens, usually on flat surface.

MOUNTAIN REEDBUCK: 12–14 mm. Scattered heaps throughout home range.

STEENBOK: 7–10 mm. Only antelope that fully buries its droppings.

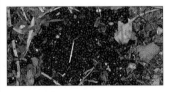

CAPE GRYSBOK: 10 mm. Communal latrines, may measure up to 1 m across.

DAMARA DIK-DIK: 7 mm. Always in communal middens.

RED DUIKER: 9 mm. Several heaps in tight clusters.

COMMON DUIKER: 11 mm. Concentrated heaps in loose middens.

SAVANNA BABOON: Variable size. Scattered, but accumulations at roosts.

VERVET MONKEY: Variable size. Scattered throughout home range.

PORCUPINE: 40–70 mm. Dropped in clusters of joined pellets, at random. Rarely in middens.

SPRINGHARE: 15–20 mm. Somewhat flattened. Small, scattered heaps.

CAPE HARE: 10 mm in diameter. Lozenge-shaped. Scattered heaps.

SMITH'S RED ROCK RABBIT: 10–15 mm in diameter. Lozenge-shaped. Large, concentrated middens.

ROCK HYRAX: 10 mm. Always in large, communal middens.

YELLOW-SPOTTED ROCK HYRAX: 10 mm in diameter. In large middens close to shelter.

DASSIE RAT: 10 mm. In small middens; dried white urine streaks also visible.

SOUTHERN AFRICAN HEDGEHOG: < 10 mm in diameter. Scattered throughout home range.

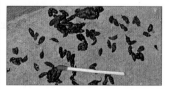

KAROO BUSH RAT: 10 mm. Deposited on stick platforms on lodges.

CAPE CLAWLESS OTTER:
22–30 mm in diameter. Lightens with age. Midden close to water.

SPOTTED-NECKED OTTER:
12–15 mm in diameter. Concentrated midden always next to water.

WATER MONGOOSE: 20 mm in diameter. Always dropped in latrines, concentrated or spread over 2 m².

DWARF MONGOOSE: 8 mm in diameter. In small middens close to den.

WHITE-TAILED MONGOOSE:
18 mm in diameter. Scattered and in loose middens.

YELLOW MONGOOSE: 12–15 mm in diameter. In concentrated middens close to warrens.

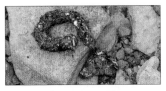

SMALL-SPOTTED GENET: 15 mm in diameter. Usually in compact middens; sometimes scattered.

AFRICAN CIVET: Variable size. Always in middens – 'civetries'.

BAT-EARED FOX: 18 mm in diameter. Often in concentrated middens at dens; also scattered.

BLACK-BACKED JACKAL: 20 mm in diameter. Scattered throughout home range; often on top of bush.

SPOTTED HYAENA: 30–40 mm in diameter. Scattered and in loose middens. Whitens with age.

BROWN HYAENA: 30–45 mm in diameter. Middens more concentrated than those of spotted hyaena.

AARDWOLF: 40–50 mm in diameter. In concentrated middens, each in 'trough'.

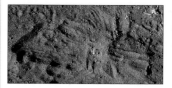

AFRICAN WILDCAT: 12–15 mm in diameter. Nearly always buried; scattered.

CARACAL: 20 mm in diameter. Scattered at random through home range.

CHEETAH: 25–35 mm in diameter. Scattered, but also concentrations at 'play trees'.

LION: > 40 mm in diameter. Scattered, never in middens.

LEOPARD: 20–30 mm in diameter. Deposited at random, also loose middens at crossroads.

FRUIT BAT: Very liquid splashes; frequently on walls of buildings.

EGYPTIAN FREE-TAILED BAT: 8 mm. Scattered and concentrated at roosts.

TRACK COMPARISONS

HANDS & FEET

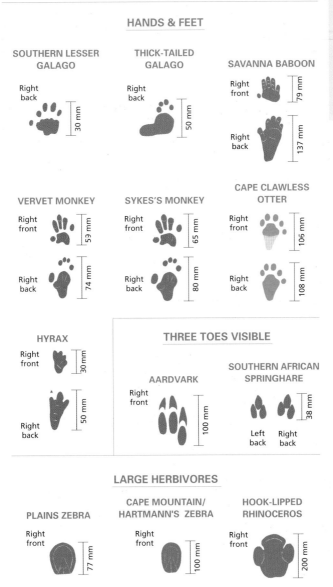

SOUTHERN LESSER GALAGO

Right back

30 mm

THICK-TAILED GALAGO

Right back

50 mm

SAVANNA BABOON

Right front

79 mm

Right back

137 mm

VERVET MONKEY

Right front

53 mm

Right back

74 mm

SYKES'S MONKEY

Right front

65 mm

Right back

80 mm

CAPE CLAWLESS OTTER

Right front

105 mm

Right back

108 mm

HYRAX

Right front

30 mm

Right back

50 mm

THREE TOES VISIBLE

AARDVARK

Right front

100 mm

SOUTHERN AFRICAN SPRINGHARE

38 mm

Left back

Right back

LARGE HERBIVORES

PLAINS ZEBRA

Right front

77 mm

CAPE MOUNTAIN/ HARTMANN'S ZEBRA

Right front

100 mm

HOOK-LIPPED RHINOCEROS

Right front

200 mm

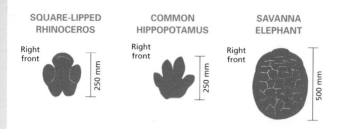

SQUARE-LIPPED RHINOCEROS

Right front

250 mm

COMMON HIPPOPOTAMUS

Right front

250 mm

SAVANNA ELEPHANT

Right front

500 mm

EVEN-TOED HOOVED ANIMALS

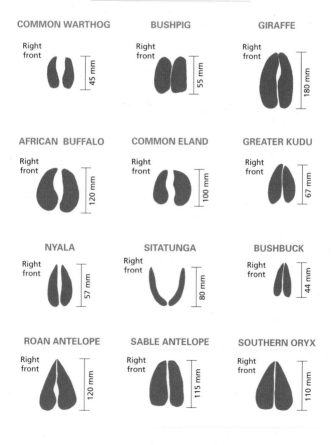

COMMON WARTHOG

Right front

45 mm

BUSHPIG

Right front

55 mm

GIRAFFE

Right front

180 mm

AFRICAN BUFFALO

Right front

120 mm

COMMON ELAND

Right front

100 mm

GREATER KUDU

Right front

67 mm

NYALA

Right front

57 mm

SITATUNGA

Right front

80 mm

BUSHBUCK

Right front

44 mm

ROAN ANTELOPE

Right front

120 mm

SABLE ANTELOPE

Right front

115 mm

SOUTHERN ORYX

Right front

110 mm

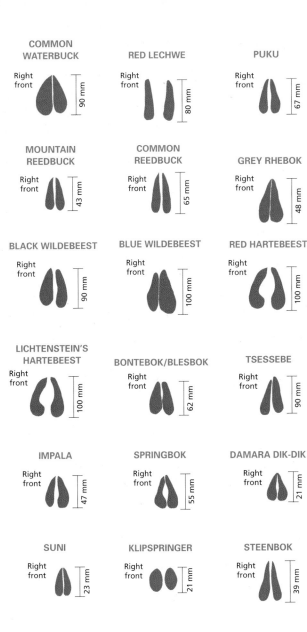

COMMON WATERBUCK
Right front
90 mm

RED LECHWE
Right front
80 mm

PUKU
Right front
67 mm

MOUNTAIN REEDBUCK
Right front
43 mm

COMMON REEDBUCK
Right front
65 mm

GREY RHEBOK
Right front
48 mm

BLACK WILDEBEEST
Right front
90 mm

BLUE WILDEBEEST
Right front
100 mm

RED HARTEBEEST
Right front
100 mm

LICHTENSTEIN'S HARTEBEEST
Right front
100 mm

BONTEBOK/BLESBOK
Right front
62 mm

TSESSEBE
Right front
90 mm

IMPALA
Right front
47 mm

SPRINGBOK
Right front
55 mm

DAMARA DIK-DIK
Right front
21 mm

SUNI
Right front
23 mm

KLIPSPRINGER
Right front
21 mm

STEENBOK
Right front
39 mm

ORIBI
Right front
40 mm

CAPE GRYSBOK
Right front
34 mm

SHARPE'S GRYSBOK
Right front
25 mm

RED DUIKER
Right front
30 mm

BLUE DUIKER
Right front
24 mm

COMMON DUIKER
Right front
42 mm

PAWS WITH CLAWS

CAPE FOX
Right front
40 mm without claws

BAT-EARED FOX
Right front
36 mm without claws

BLACK-BACKED JACKAL
Right front
51 mm without claws

SIDE-STRIPED JACKAL
Right front
43 mm without claws

AFRICAN WILD DOG
Right front
70 mm without claws

SPOTTED-NECKED OTTER
Right front
58 mm without claws

HONEY BADGER
Right front
58 mm without claws

STRIPED POLECAT
Right front
22 mm without claws

BANDED MONGOOSE
Right front
29 mm without claws

SMALL GREY MONGOOSE
Right front
25 mm without claws

SLENDER MONGOOSE
Right front
23 mm without claws

WHITE-TAILED MONGOOSE
Right front
41 mm without claws

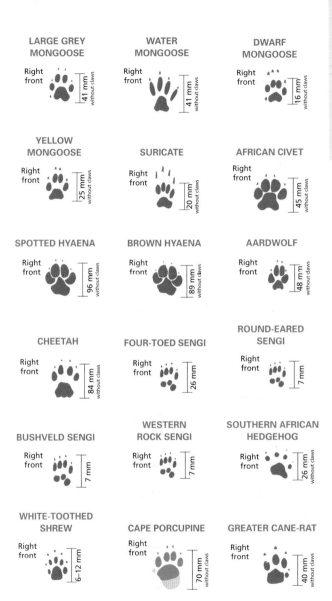

LARGE GREY MONGOOSE
Right front
41 mm without claws

WATER MONGOOSE
Right front
41 mm without claws

DWARF MONGOOSE
Right front
16 mm without claws

YELLOW MONGOOSE
Right front
25 mm without claws

SURICATE
Right front
20 mm without claws

AFRICAN CIVET
Right front
45 mm without claws

SPOTTED HYAENA
Right front
96 mm without claws

BROWN HYAENA
Right front
89 mm without claws

AARDWOLF
Right front
48 mm without claws

CHEETAH
Right front
84 mm without claws

FOUR-TOED SENGI
Right front
26 mm

ROUND-EARED SENGI
Right front
7 mm

BUSHVELD SENGI
Right front
7 mm

WESTERN ROCK SENGI
Right front
7 mm

SOUTHERN AFRICAN HEDGEHOG
Right front
26 mm without claws

WHITE-TOOTHED SHREW
Right front
6–12 mm

CAPE PORCUPINE
Right front
70 mm without claws

GREATER CANE-RAT
Right front
40 mm without claws

145

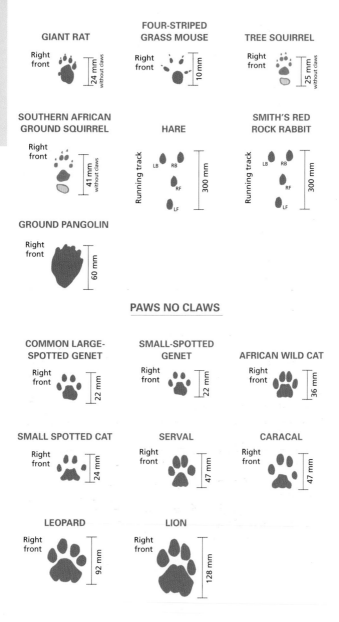

GIANT RAT

Right front

24 mm without claws

FOUR-STRIPED GRASS MOUSE

Right front

10 mm

TREE SQUIRREL

Right front

25 mm without claws

SOUTHERN AFRICAN GROUND SQUIRREL

Right front

41 mm without claws

HARE

Running track

LB · RB

RF

LF

300 mm

SMITH'S RED ROCK RABBIT

Running track

LB · RB

RF

LF

300 mm

GROUND PANGOLIN

Right front

60 mm

PAWS NO CLAWS

COMMON LARGE-SPOTTED GENET

Right front

22 mm

SMALL-SPOTTED GENET

Right front

22 mm

AFRICAN WILD CAT

Right front

36 mm

SMALL SPOTTED CAT

Right front

24 mm

SERVAL

Right front

47 mm

CARACAL

Right front

47 mm

LEOPARD

Right front

92 mm

LION

Right front

128 mm

GLOSSARY

Aestivate To enter a state of torpor in summer.

Aquatic Living mainly, or entirely, in water.

Arboreal Living in trees.

Boss The area at the top of the head where horns are at their thickest and heaviest, e.g. as in savanna buffalo and blue wildebeest.

Browser An animal that eats shoots and leaves of trees, bushes and shrubs.

Carnivore Meat-eating animal.

Crepuscular Active at twilight.

Diurnal Active during daylight hours.

Erectile Capable of being raised to an erect position.

Farrow (of a sow) To give birth to a litter of piglets.

Fluke Either of the two lobes of a whale's tail.

Foraging Searching for food.

Form Shallow depression or nest in which a hare lives.

Fossorial Living underground.

Gestation Period of development of young within the uterus; conception to birth.

Grazer An animal that eats grasses.

Grizzled Streaked with grey, black or white hairs.

Home range Area in which an animal normally lives and carries out its day-to-day activities.

Inguinal Relating to, or situated in, the groin region.

Midden Place where droppings/scats are regularly deposited.

Nocturnal Active during the hours of darkness.

Oestrus Period during which female mammal is sexually receptive to males.

Omnivore Animal with a varied diet that includes both animals and plants.

Rut Period of sexual excitement in males; associated with mating season.

Sounder Collective name for pigs.

Species Group of interbreeding individuals of common ancestry, reproductively isolated from other groups.

Terrestrial Living on land.

Territory Area defended from intruders by an individual or group.

SUGGESTED FURTHER READING

Skinner, J.D. & Chimimba, C.T. 2005. *The Mammals of the Southern African Subregion*. Cambridge University Press, Cambridge.

Stuart, Chris & Tilde. 2001. *A Field Guide to the Tracks and Signs of Southern and East African Wildlife*. Struik Publishers, Cape Town.

Stuart, Chris & Tilde. 2007. *Field Guide to Mammals of Southern Africa*. Struik Publishers, Cape Town.

Stuart, Chris & Tilde. 2006. *Field Guide to the Larger Mammals of Africa*. Struik Publishers, Cape Town.

Stuart, Chris & Tilde. 2009. *Pocket Guide: Mammals of East Africa*. Random House Struik, Cape Town.

Square-lipped rhino

ACKNOWLEDGEMENTS

We would like to thank those who helped fill our photographic blanks, as listed under photographic credits, and our friend Galen Rathbun (California Academy of Sciences) for coming up with the phrase 'flute snoots' for the sengis. Also to Jane Hoepfl, thanks for trapping rodents and her dedication to the bush Karoo rats. Special thanks go to Pippa Parker of Random House Struik, for suggesting the title, and to the rest of the team: Helen de Villiers, Colette Alves, Janice Evans and Jennifer Addington, for pulling it all together.

PHOTOGRAPHIC CREDITS

Brett Atkins: p 132; **Duncan Butchart:** pp 11, 86; **Tony Camacho/Images of Africa:** p 74; **John Carlyon:** pp 60, 104; **Mark Carwardine:** p 133; **Roger de la Harpe/Images of Africa:** back cover, top; **Gallo/Getty Images:** p 134; **Martin Harvey/ Images of Africa:** front cover; **Ian Manning:** p 27 (inset); **M.G.L. (Gus) Mills:** p 79; **Brent Moseley Naudé:** p 117; **Harald Nicolay:** p 75 (inset); **John Phielix/Images of Africa:** p 131; **Galen Rathburn:** p 92; **Alex Sliwa:** p 82; **A. Tranter:** p 102; **Lara Tranter:** p 137 (b); **Ariadne van Zandbergen/Images of Africa:** p 41; **John Visser:** p 10; **Hein von Horsten/Images of Africa:** back cover, fourth from top

INDEXES

SCIENTIFIC NAMES

AFRIKAANS COMMON NAMES

FRENCH COMMON NAMES

ENGLISH COMMON NAMES